Serving without sinking

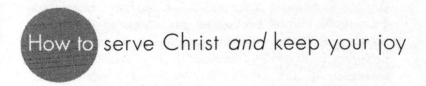

How to serve Christ *and* keep your joy

John Hindley

To my wife, Flick.
Your love, fun, wisdom and kindness make our
marriage a delightful gift from Christ to me.

Serving without sinking: *How to serve Christ and keep your joy*
© John Hindley/The Good Book Company, 2013. Reprinted 2013, 2014.

Published by
The Good Book Company
Tel (UK): 0333 123 0880;
International: +44 (0) 208 942 0880
Email: info@thegoodbook.co.uk

Websites:
UK: www.thegoodbook.co.uk
North America: www.thegoodbook.com
Australia: www.thegoodbook.com.au
New Zealand: www.thegoodbook.co.nz

ISBN: 9781908762351

Printed in the UK
Design by André Parker

Contents

1. Introduction

Martin began to relax as he walked home from church. His work was finished. He'd opened up, sorted out the chairs, done the children's talk, and cleared away afterwards. He felt free—he'd done his duty and now the rest of the day was his. He could relax and enjoy himself. What a wonderful feeling!

Sophie had been running the children's holiday club at church. It had been exhausting, and the clear-up had finished her off. Just as she collapsed onto the sofa, the phone rang. It was a guy from church. Could she get the bread for communion the next morning? It would only be a ten-minute walk. She said yes, of course—but inside she was seething. Furious with... well, with Jesus. She'd been serving Him all week; she'd been the only one who stayed behind to clear up; everyone else was relaxing at home; *she* had to go and get the bread. Couldn't He give her a break?

David really loved his new church. The harvest supper had been great—he was starting to make friends. Afterwards, the pastor asked him to help put some stage blocks back in the storage loft. He joined a group of guys lifting them in. It was great fun and a good laugh—and afterwards the pastor thanked him for being an example of joyful service. David went home praising God. He liked serving Christ. He was going to enjoy being part of this church.

Brad had been a student for three years when it all clicked. The minister was preaching on God's love, and particularly God's love in dying for those who were so flawed. Something happened that night in his heart—and he knew that all he wanted to do was serve Him. He fixed up a meeting the next day with the minister, and told him he wanted to spend his life serving Jesus—and that he wanted help to get started.

I have been all those people (I gave myself different names, and in one case a different gender!). And I have gone through those feelings in reverse order, from Brad through David to Sophie and Martin. This book comes out of what had happened in my soul, that turned serving Jesus from the thing I enjoyed most into a chore that I resented and a duty I had to fulfil.

Maybe you feel the same. Maybe you remember a time when serving Jesus was exciting, something you wanted to do—but now it's something you just have to do. The busy-ness has sucked out the joy—it's a constant battle to keep your head above water. *A servant is who you have to be.*

Maybe for you it's not like that. Perhaps for you, serving is nothing like a duty; it's your glory. You see yourself as, and you love that everyone else sees you as, a dependable volunteer; or an admired children's-group teacher; or a well-respected preacher. *A servant is who you are.*

Or perhaps you work hard behind the scenes at your church—and no one ever notices. You can feel yourself growing bitter about serving because it's never met with a thank-you. *A servant is who you'd like people to notice you are.*

Maybe you serve as much as you can, because you want to be as good a Christian as you can. Otherwise, God's not going to bless you, is He? Sometimes you go to work without reading your Bible and praying, and you know the day will go badly—God won't be pleased with someone as useless as you. *A servant is who God demands you be.*

Or perhaps you are none of those people. You don't need to run around serving Jesus—the whole point of Christianity is that you're saved by grace! He's done it all so that you don't have to. He's given you your ticket to heaven. *A servant is not who you need to be.*

Maybe you're not a Christian and you have some questions. Christians talk about freedom and forgiveness. They talk about a God who loves and asks nothing in return. Then they live as though working for the most demanding, picky, small-minded of gods.

The thing is that Christians serve for many kinds of reasons—and almost all of them are flawed. I know my motives are mixed at best, wrong at worst.

Christian service shouldn't leave us feeling irritated, exhausted, guilty, proud, bitter or lazy—but all too often I chat to Christians who feel one (or all!) of those things. I see them in myself, too.

So this book looks at our service. When we think of serving as Christians, we often think of what we do for and with church; and so the majority of the examples and applications in each chapter are about serving as part of our churches. Our service of Jesus is much wider than this, though, and maybe when you think of serving Him, you most naturally focus on another area of service—in your home, bringing up children, or in someone else's home, looking after an elderly relative or friend, or somewhere else. Christian service is not less than what we do on Sundays at church, but it's much more than that. So wherever and however you are serving, the truths in this book apply.

But this book isn't primarily about *our* service. It's mainly about Jesus Christ, and about *His* service. He said that He "did not come to be served, but to serve, and to give his life as a ransom for many" (Mark 10 v 45). He meant it. He was taken, beaten, tried, mocked, nailed, hung, cursed, judged, killed. He served. He loved.

So Jesus does not want you to measure your life by your service of Him. He does not want your service to get in the way of your love for Him. He did not come to be served by you—He came to serve you.

If we grasp this, then we will be set free to enjoy His love. And then, oddly, we will also be set free to serve Him longer, harder, braver, truer than we ever could otherwise. This is joy, and we'll only find it in Christ.

I was all four of those people (including Sophie). I still am, at times. I pray that this book helps you in your love for Jesus, your joy in Jesus, and then—and only then—with your service of Jesus. And at this point in writing, I'm praying it does that for me, too!

2. Serving can be joyful

I often feel weary, discouraged or bitter in serving Jesus. These are not just past realities for me. This is a realistic summary of my heart most days. I don't think it's just me—I see signs of it in my Christian friends, too. We often seem to be a burdened, joyless bunch. It should not be like this, and it doesn't need to be—for me or for you.

If you're a Christian, you believe that Jesus is the ultimately loving and powerful King, the Christ. And you believe that He is the perfect Son of God, through whom all things were created. So what should it be like to work for Him? Surely Jesus should be the boss that everyone dreams of. Yet from the way most of us Christians go about serving Him, you'd be more likely to think He was a cross between Montgomery Burns from *The Simpsons* and David Brent or Michael Scott from *The Office* (depending on whether you watch the UK or US version!).

We often subconsciously feel, and then live, like there is a disconnect between the promises that Jesus makes to us in His Bible, and the way it actually works out when we follow Him. Let me show you what I mean. In Matthew 11 v 28 Jesus makes an amazing promise:

> Come to me, all you who are weary and burdened, and I will give you rest.

An enticing promise

I love the feel of this promise. It appeals on so many levels. Think back to times when you have worked hard. Perhaps your job is one of physical toil. Maybe your daily work is looking after a home or children with all the tiredness that comes from that. Perhaps your work (like mine) is mainly at a desk—if so, think back to a long day in the garden, or moving house. There is a simple pleasure to the end of a time of hard work, when you can sit down with a mug of tea or pint of beer and relax. When toil is over and rest begins. This promise captures the satisfaction of that moment.

It goes deeper than that, too. Jesus calls to Him those who are "weary". Weariness is the mixture of tiredness and despondency. It is when you have worked hard at a task that seems unending, and then you stand staring at the mountain of work still to do. Weariness is what you feel in your bones during a long illness, where good health is a faint memory and something you fear you will never recapture. Weariness is getting home with no idea of how to make your relationship with your husband or wife or child happy again. Weariness is turning up to the church prayer meeting because that's what you do, hoping it doesn't overrun, looking forward to getting home and falling into bed.

It is right into this weariness that Jesus speaks. Into the burdens of life—of pain, sadness, illness, weakness, sin, failure, guilt, shame—Jesus speaks. He gives a wonderfully simple promise:

Come to me... and I will give you rest.

He promises everything we hope for. Everything our hearts cry for. Jesus is our God. He sees all the weariness in our hearts, all the burdens we carry that no one else has a clue about. He sees the worries on our minds. He sees the stress of our lives. He looks us in the eye and He says: *Come here, to me. I will give you rest from all that. I know, I understand, and I came to make it better; I came to give you rest.*

That entices me. The simple depth of His promise makes me want it. The offer of rest when I so often feel weary draws me. My heart cries: *Yes, Lord.*

But then my mind says: *Really? That isn't what coming to Jesus is really like, is it, John? Not really.*

An empty promise?

I question this promise because it doesn't feel as if it stacks up to how life has been since I began to follow Jesus. So many of the weary burdens of life seem to be just the same. My Christian friends don't seem to have it any easier either, so I don't think it's just me. Jobs are just as hard; relationships have as much potential to cause hurt; illness and death cause as much pain.

I am drawn to this promise of Jesus, but deep down I am not sure I believe Him. Or more accurately, I only half believe Him. Because I feel weary and burdened now, and not restful, I assume that Jesus must be talking about the future, when He returns to this world. Slog now: satisfaction later. Work hard now, because it'll be worth it later. Presumably that's why the apostle Paul says: "I consider that our present sufferings are not worth comparing with the glory that will be revealed in us" (Romans 8 v 18). We suffer now, but we'll get glory later, when Christ comes back.

There is definitely something right in this. We suffer terribly, and the heart-cry of the suffering church through the ages is "Come, Lord Jesus" (Revelation 22 v 20).

But if this is the nature of the rest Jesus promises, we've got a couple of problems. First, if He is offering rest later, if you carry your burdens between now and then, it seems a little deceptive to shout to a crowd: "Come to me ... and I will give you rest". Surely He is implying that He will help now, not just in many years' time?

Second, when we come to Jesus, He actually seems to increase our burdens. If Jesus is really, finally and ultimately about offering us rest, then it seems strange that He would add to our weariness now. Yet isn't that often how it feels? Have you ever got to the end of the week and wished you had two days to do whatever you wanted? Thought how nice it would be to sleep late *twice* at the weekend? Envied your co-workers who get to lie on a beach when you are off to help at a Christian camp for teenagers? Or totalled up your giving over the year and then thought, as you begin your "staycation", of where you could have gone if you'd spent the money you earned on yourself?

The Lord Jesus calls us to be holy; to tell the whole world about Him; to love our fellow Christians, and our neighbours. He tells us to give our money, time, efforts and hopes to Him, in His service. It just doesn't feel as if He means it when He promises to remove our burdens and give us rest. It feels as though He piles a few more burdens onto our shoulders.

A strings-attached non-promise?

Perhaps this shouldn't surprise us—just after the offer of "rest", Jesus seems to add the strings. The whole of His offer in Matthew 11 v 28-30 goes like this:

> Come to me, all you who are weary and burdened, and I will give you rest. Take my yoke upon you and learn from me, for

I am gentle and humble in heart, and you will find rest for
your souls. For my yoke is easy and my burden is light.

He promises rest, and then says He will yoke us! Just as
animals are yoked to pull a plough, Jesus says that to accept His
offer is to agree to be yoked to His service. So maybe there are
some strings attached after all! Maybe we shouldn't expect too
much. Maybe we should just get our heads down now, get on
with it, slog out our time here and hope that following Jesus will
be a better experience when He comes back than it is now.

We see this as a contradiction. We hear "rest" and "yoke", and
deep down we believe only one of the parts of this promise is
true. We either work hard for Jesus, seeing church as a chore
that we just need to get on with, muttering about those who don't
do much to help. Or we put our feet up and smile at the futile
efforts of those workaholic brothers and sisters who work all
hours as we turn up to the service twenty minutes late, coffee in
hand. Or, if you're like me, you live in a conflicted, contradictory
world where you're working as though your salvation depended
on it one day, and lazing around the next. Some of us rest easy;
some wear a heavy yoke. Some of us alternate between the two.

But Jesus isn't giving us a contradictory promise. He is offering
rest *and* yoke. Both, now. Whether we're slaving or lazy, we all
get it wrong, because Jesus offers a restful yoke—His "yoke is
easy and [His] burden is light".

How can that work? What does this look like? And have you
ever actually experienced it?

Deep down, I wonder if Jesus is mistaken, or unrealistic. But
when I feel that following Jesus is a burden, either He got it
wrong or I did. And He is God—He has never lied or made a
mistake. This means that my experience is wrong; that following
Jesus can be, and is meant to be, easy and light. Working for

Him is meant to be a joy. Of course, we will only experience this fully when He comes back, but we should taste it now. We should see and feel that He lifts our burdens, hefts them over His shoulder and lugs them up the hill for us. We should be able to say to our friends: *Come to Jesus, commit your life to His cause, and He will give you rest*—and mean it.

And we should be able to say it to ourselves, too—and mean it. Working for this Boss can be, and should be, restful, joyful, wonderful.

So why isn't it?

3. A wrong view of God

It's 9.30am at Holy Trinity Church in Genericville. The service won't start till 10.30am, but there are already some church members in the building. The Smiths are setting up the coffee table. The Sanchez family are folding the service sheets. The Smalls are preparing to teach a children's group.

All are serving. Their hands are busy—too busy, they all sometimes feel. But are they serving Christianly? They may be; or they may not be. When it comes to Christian service, the first place to look is at what is going on in our hearts, not what we are doing with our hands.

So this chapter and the next one explore what might be happening as we think about serving and get on with serving, uncovering the wrong motives which leave us so burdened and miserable and joyless. We can get it wrong by having a wrong view of God; or by having a wrong view of people, both of others and of ourselves. This chapter is about how we get our view of Jesus wrong. In the next chapter, we'll see how we get our view of people wrong.

You might not see yourself in each of the sections in these next two chapters. I am afraid that all of them apply to me, some more commonly or clearly than others. If you don't spot yourself in every one of these categories, praise God—there's no need to search the depths of your heart for mistakes you are not making!

If you do find yourself nodding along with a sinking feeling, then don't despair—there is a lot of good news to come in a couple of chapters' time.

Serving Jesus... to be good enough for Him

"Jesus wants me to be good, to obey Him. I know He died for me, to give me the chance to go to heaven. Now I've got to make sure I'm good enough to continue to earn His forgiveness, to keep my place in heaven. That's a great motivation for working hard for Him and His people!"

Jesus once told a story about two men who found themselves praying near one another:

To some who were confident of their own righteousness and looked down on everybody else, Jesus told this parable: "Two men went up to the temple to pray, one a Pharisee and the other a tax collector. The Pharisee stood up and prayed about himself: 'God, I thank you that I am not like other men—robbers, evildoers, adulterers—or even like this tax collector. I fast twice a week and give a tenth of all I get.'

"But the tax collector stood at a distance. He would not even look up to heaven, but beat his breast and said, 'God, have mercy on me, a sinner.'

"I tell you that this man, rather than the other, went home justified before God. For everyone who exalts himself will be humbled, and he who humbles himself will be exalted."

(Luke 18 v 9-14)

Some people try to serve Jesus because they think He only likes good people. They are trying to make themselves good enough for Him to accept them in the first place, or (more subtly, and therefore more dangerously) to stay good enough for Him to keep forgiving them. After all, if we want to be friends with a holy, perfect God, we need to clean our act up, don't we? "I am the LORD your God; consecrate yourselves and be holy, because I am holy" (Leviticus 11 v 44). God wants us to be holy, and so we try hard, work hard, serve hard.

This Pharisee in Jesus' story was like that. We can instinctively (and a little ironically!) look down on him for looking down on the tax collector. But let's give the guy a break. He is humble— he doesn't think his goodness is all his own achievement, so he thanks God for it. He is committed to God, fasting for two days a week. He is generous to others, giving a tenth of his income away. He is simply working hard to be holy like his God. And he's doing well.

So what's his problem? It's that he thinks he has made it. That's why he thanks the Lord that he is "not like other men" (Luke 18 v 11). He has divided the world in two. There are those, like the tax collector, who are not accepted by God because they don't do enough for Him, and there are those, like him, who are. He thinks that the good things he has done have put him in the category of the people God thinks are good enough. He thinks he has "justified" himself—made himself righteous, right with God.

Then Jesus throws a tub of icy water on the cosy assumption of all rule-keeping religious systems; on the view that if we do good things, God counts us as righteous. He turns to the tax collector, a first-century con-man who knew his flaws so clearly that he "would not even look up to heaven", and says of him: "I tell you that this man, rather than the other, went home justified before God" (v 13-14).

This good Pharisee was not justified; the wicked tax collector was. The group of righteous people includes the tax collector but does not include the Pharisee. How can this be?

The reason is that we can never live up to God's goodness. Jesus is always generous and loving, and we are regularly selfish and cold towards Him and others. Think back to that verse from Leviticus. Can we *really* be as holy as Jesus?! At the very best, this is going to lead us to terrible uncertainty. Can you imagine looking back at the end of the day and thinking: *Now, how many minutes today was I as loving as Christ? Have I done enough?* It sounds silly when put like that, but it's the question that anyone who relies on their own service to justify themselves has to ask, all the time. And we can never do enough. The Pharisee had tried everything he could in his quest to be good. Jesus' verdict? Not enough, not righteous, not justified.

Serving Jesus to become good enough for Him might sound noble; in fact, it is futile. It is a recipe for constant doubt over whether we've done enough for Him, and so for uncertainty and misery... and failure.

When we get ourselves into this mindset, we do one of three things. First, we might re-invent Jesus; construct our own Jesus to suit our needs. We decide that Jesus will smile at us as long as we do our best. But to worship a made-up Jesus is a disaster. A made-up Jesus isn't any Jesus—He can't hear, can't help, can't open heaven to you. If you serve Jesus in order to be, or to stay, saved, it's a dangerous place to be. Remember, that Pharisee thought he was one of God's most faithful friends. Jesus said he did not know God at all. That's meant to shock us, to provoke us to ask: *Am I in any way like that Pharisee?*

Second, we might not re-invent Jesus. We might understand just how perfect He is, and see how imperfect even our best moments, even our greatest works for Him, are. And then we'll despair. We'll give up.

Third, we may realise that the real Jesus is kinder than any false imitation we can imagine. And we'll bring to Him not our resumé of service, but our request for undeserved forgiveness: "God, have mercy on me, a sinner." We'll love knowing that "this [type of] man, rather than the other, went home justified before God".

And we'll stop thinking of our service as being what keeps us friends with Jesus.

Serving Jesus… to get something from Him

"God is the Giver of all good things. And He blesses us as we serve Him. So if I work hard for Him, then He'll be good to me, won't He? So I read my Bible, I pray, and I do lots at church."

In Luke 15, Christ tells a series of stories to show that God loves to find lost people (people like that tax collector) and bring them back to Him. He compares God to a shepherd who finds a lost sheep, a lady who finds a lost coin, and a father who finds a lost son. This last story is more detailed than the others; there is a second son.

We will pick the story up at the point where the younger brother—who has treated his father as though he were dead, spent all his inheritance, and only then realised that life without his father simply doesn't work—has just come home to apologise:

The father said to his servants, "Quick! Bring the best robe and put it on him. Put a ring on his finger and sandals on his feet. Bring the fattened calf and kill it. Let's have a feast and celebrate. For this son of mine was dead and is alive again; he was lost and is found." So they began to celebrate.

Meanwhile, the older son was in the field. When he came near the house, he heard music and dancing. So he called one of the servants and asked him what was going on. "Your brother has come," he replied, "and your father has killed the fattened calf because he has him back safe and sound."

The older brother became angry and refused to go in. So his father went out and pleaded with him. But he answered his father, "Look! All these years I've been slaving for you and never disobeyed your orders. Yet you never gave me even a young goat so I could celebrate with my friends. But when this son of yours who has squandered your property with prostitutes comes home, you kill the fattened calf for him!"

"My son," the father said, "you are always with me, and everything I have is yours. But we had to celebrate and be glad, because this brother of yours was dead and is alive again; he was lost and is found."   (Luke 15 v 22-32)

This older brother is a good guy. He is loyal, dependable. You can imagine that he is seen as a pillar of the community, a chip off the old block. Not like his loser brother, running off to squander the family wealth on sex and drugs and rock and roll.

But underneath, his heart is as selfish as his brother's. His younger brother hated his father and just wanted his money. He took the cash and ran, only coming back when he had spent the lot and the good times were over. The older brother is just the same; he wants a goat! Both brothers want their father's gifts, and not their father himself; they simply have different ways of getting those gifts. The older brother wants to deserve blessing.

He wants to put his father in his debt, to work hard so that his father has to bless him. He wants his father to owe it to him. The older brother doesn't love his father—he only works hard because he wants a pay-cheque.

Jesus told this story to a group that included "tax collectors and sinners" (15 v 1)—younger brothers who'd enjoyed God's world while rejecting Him. But the group also included "the Pharisees and teachers of the law" (v 2), religious people who would never dream of running away from serving God—older brothers. The shock is that they don't love God either—they only serve him to get good stuff from Him. They love the gifts, not the Giver. They love the blessings, but they don't love God.

Let's think about how this might play out for us. Sometimes it is expressed hopefully. I long to see my church grow so I will work hard at praying, being good, teaching the Bible. These things are faithful service of Christ, and if I do them, He will surely make the church grow large and happy... won't He?

Sometimes it is expressed fearfully. Before leaving for work, I knew I should read my Bible and pray—but today I got out of bed late and then surfed the web. Now I'm walking into a big meeting, and I know it will go badly. I've done nothing for Jesus today, so He won't come through for me now.

Other times, it is expressed bitterly. I worked hard, I led a Bible study, I was the first to volunteer for jobs at church. I prayed for missionaries and for the sick. And I have prayed and prayed for a child, but we don't have one yet. *I did my bit, Jesus, and You owe me. You haven't come through; You have cheated me.*

When I think like this, I'm not thinking Christianly; I'm opting for pagan religion. In the ancient world, if I were a merchant going on a voyage, before my ship left harbour I would kill a goat and pour its blood into the sea as a gift to the god of the sea. I would serve him, do what he wanted, so that he would give me a good voyage and favourable winds. *Here's the goat, sea god. Do we have a deal? Yup, we got a deal.*

Jesus is generous, and He is powerful. He is also a person, and when we treat Him as a deal to be closed, an official to be bought or a chump to be flattered, He doesn't like it. It is deeply offensive.

If I want to have some friends round on Saturday night to watch a film that involves swords, battles and bad dialogue, I might ask my wife, Flick (who, for some reason, doesn't enjoy that kind of film—there's no accounting for taste!), if that fits with her plans. Or I might buy her flowers, take her out for dinner and *then* ask. I might figure I am much more likely to get the answer I want if I show her a bit of kindness first.

But actually, if I stop and think about it, that's pretty manipulative, isn't it? I'm only doing nice things for her so that she'll let me do what I want. My "kindness" is actually selfish! And I'm treating her as though she's a bit stingy—as though she'll never be good to me unless I've already been good to her. Behind my apparent kindness, I am manipulating her and treating her as though she doesn't love me. If she realised what I was doing, it would break her heart.

And it's so easy to treat God like that. We need to forget the idea that God is pleased with things we do just because we do them; that He gives blessings in proportion to our service, as though the imaginary god wants blood, and the real God wants sweat; as though if we pitch up early for church, set up the sound system and then stay late to pack it up, Jesus will give us what we want in life.

Of course Jesus is pleased when we do what He has asked because we love Him. But it is the *love* He most cares about, not the *service*. Hebrews 11 v 6 says something simple, but which has staggering implications:

> Without faith it is impossible to please God.

Faith is "being sure of what we hope for" (v 1)—it is trust in Jesus and all He lovingly promises us. Faith is confidence that in finding Jesus, we have received all God's "rewards" (v 6). So if I serve Christ because I trust Him and so do as He asks, it pleases Him. But if I do as Christ asks to earn the reward of His blessing, so that He'll owe me something good, I'm getting it horribly wrong. If I do something Christ asks to make Him more loving towards me, rather than trusting that He already loves me, I have sinned.

If I'm honest, that means that a lot of what I've done in my life that I called "serving Jesus", and which looked like "serving Jesus", in fact displeased Jesus—it was sin. Each time I come back to this it shocks and humbles me. It shows me as I really am, and moves me to cry out again: *Have mercy on me, a sinner.*

We can so easily fall into thinking Jesus will love and bless us if we do the right things. Then it's a short step to feeling He owes us. And then it's not long before we decide He's let us down.

Serving Jesus... to pay Him back

> *"I know I can't pay Jesus back for what He did for me. He doesn't owe me—I owe Him, big time! But I can start. I am in His debt, and so I give my life to Him as He gave His to me, just to repay a little of what He did for me."*

Some people will *never* buy the first drink—they are hoping not to have to buy any at all, making it a cheap evening. Others *always* buy the first drink, and then make sure they get another round in later—they are hoping to avoid owing anyone.

Most of us don't like being in debt. If we are in debt, we look forward to paying it back. If we have a big debt, like a mortgage, we plan to pay it back bit by bit. But when we apply that to our relationship with God and our service of God, we get into a mess!

> If I speak in the tongues of men and of angels, but have not love, I am only a resounding gong or a clanging cymbal. If I have the gift of prophecy and can fathom all mysteries and all knowledge, and if I have a faith that can move mountains, but have not love, I am nothing. If I give all I possess to the poor and surrender my body to the flames, but have not love, I gain nothing. (1 Corinthians 13 v 1-3)

If you are serving God to pay Him back, and serve Him to the point of death, the apostle Paul says here that you actually gain nothing. It is a waste. The only motivation that makes such a death echo in eternity is love. Doing anything for God motivated by anything other than love, is—startlingly—"nothing".

Trying to pay Jesus back is a common mistake, though. I have heard it taught in churches a lot; sometimes, unfortunately, by me. It often goes something like this...

> *"If I committed adultery and my husband or wife forgave me, I would be very grateful. I would then try to live as a good husband as a way of thanking her for her forgiveness. I would be less likely to betray her again because I would want to repay her kindness. I would be in her debt, and would treat her accordingly."*

Gratitude is never a stand-alone motivation for serving either a forgiving spouse or a forgiving God. Gratitude is simply a response to forgiveness. And it provokes two very different motivations for service—one of which is great, the other flawed.

Gratitude can create love, which leads to rightly-motivated service. Or it can create a feeling of indebtedness, which leads to wrongly-motivated service.

If my wife forgave my adultery, it would impress me to see such love and kindness in her character. It would amaze me that this love and kindness was directed at me, and so I would be grateful and full of love for her. I would then serve her freely in love, overflowing with thanksgiving. My gratitude to her would be part of my love for her. When we have grateful love for Jesus, we will serve Him, and this is good.

But gratitude can lead to a wrong sense of indebtedness just as easily as to a right love. This too can work as a motivation, but let's think about it more in terms of a wife forgiving her husband's adultery. If as the forgiven husband I think this way, what I am saying is that I will not be a good husband out of love, but out of guilt. I am trying to pay off a debt; I'm doing good things for my wife, but they're not to please her, but to make myself feel better. Paying off a debt is about me, not about her.

When we serve God to pay Him back, we do a few things. First, we make our service about us, not about Him. Second, we act as though He isn't really forgiving, hasn't really forgotten our sin, but that at any moment He could turn round and throw it in our faces. Third, we make ourselves equal partners with God, as though we do something that contributes to our forgiveness.

Of course, this is crazy. Jesus went through the agony and terror of hell as He died on a cross, carrying all your guilt and shame in your place. How many missionaries do you need to pray for... how many cups of tea do you need to brew... how many times must you sweep the floor... to pay that back?!

Imagine a young boy who is longing for the latest games console for Christmas. He stops and looks in the shop window every time he goes past, gazing longingly at it. His mum and dad are not well-off, and it is not cheap. So, at the beginning of October, they start saving. They stop having the Friday evening take-away meal; neither of them gets a new winter coat. At great cost to themselves, they get together enough to go and buy the games console.

On Christmas Day, the little boy opens the present of his dreams, mum and dad watching with as much excitement as their son. The little boy then goes into the kitchen and fills the sink. When they ask him why, he tells them that it's going to take a lot of washing up to pay them back for such a generous present...

What is that boy saying about his parents? That he doesn't really think they've given him a gift. That they're not really generous. That they must want something in return. That, ultimately, they don't unconditionally and self-sacrificially love him.

If I think I must pay God back, then I don't really believe His gift of salvation was free in the first place. Jesus loves to give and give and give, freely and generously. We cannot pay Him back through serving Him, and even to try to do so is to rob Him of His glory as the great Lover, the great Giver.

All these three attitudes are outworkings of the same thing: not realising, or remembering, who the real God is. They stymie our serving, and they stem from a wrong view of God:

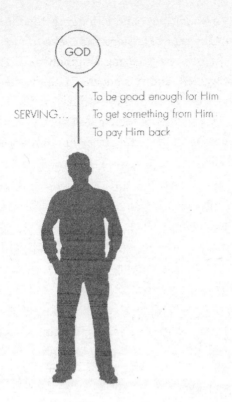

GOD

SERVING...

To be good enough for Him
To get something from Him
To pay Him back

If your heart is anything like mine, it's been a bit painful to read this chapter and recognise yourself and your own thoughts and emotions. The good news is: we're now halfway through looking at our own hearts. The bad news is: we're only halfway through!

4. A wrong view of people

The last chapter was pretty tough. This one is, too. But it's only as we realise what we need setting free from that we can appreciate the freedom Jesus offers—only as we see ourselves as we really are that we can begin to appreciate who Jesus really is.

A wrong view of others

Serving... to impress

> *"I love serving. It gives me a real buzz, and reassures me that I'm a real Christian. I love the feeling inside when someone praises me for doing something hard, or doing something well. I really like knowing that I'm seen as a mature, committed, useful Christian. It gives me security and purpose, which is what the Christian life is about."*

Jesus uses some pretty blunt language about serving to impress people in Matthew 5 – 7. He even labels this attitude hypocrisy:

> Be careful not to do your "acts of righteousness" before men, to be seen by them. If you do, you will have no reward from your Father in heaven.
> So when you give to the needy, do not announce it with

trumpets, as the hypocrites do in the synagogues and on the streets, to be honoured by men. I tell you the truth, they have received their reward in full. (Matthew 6 v 1-2)

This is strong stuff. Why is Jesus so condemning of this attitude? Because, again, it's taking something that should be about Jesus, and about others, and making it all about me.

And, I think, Jesus is so strong because this is such a subtle temptation. Enjoying encouragement is fine, but seeking it isn't—and they don't look very different.

Back in chapter one, I told you of my delight in serving Christ by helping clear up after a harvest supper. One of the pastors told me that I had been an example of joyful service. My heart was really encouraged. I had simply been enjoying myself, and to hear that I had helped others by showing them something of Christ just made me happier. I hadn't expected anyone to notice, and I wouldn't have minded if they hadn't.

What is sad is how quickly "being noticed" can become something we need, and so something we seek. Without consciously realising, we become people who need to be noticed. We want other people to think well of us. We "serve Jesus" in order, in truth, to serve our own reputation.

It's a subtle shift. One Wednesday you are working late to meet a deadline, humming to yourself happily, knowing that it is a blessing to work as one who serves Christ. You are surprised on the Thursday morning to find an email from one of the senior executives saying that she noticed you at your desk and appreciates the work you put in. At 5.30pm that evening, you see she is still in her office and decide that maybe you'll stay an extra hour or two... you move your chair slightly to make sure it's in her line of sight.

Once we begin doing good in order to be noticed, we are letting other people's opinions define us. If our church leaders, our Christian friends, our family members or our work colleagues tell us that we are good, then we are.

But, Jesus says, if we serve to be honoured by men, then that is what we will get, and all we will get: the honour of men. We will get nothing from God. He views what we are doing as hypocrisy, not service.

When we serve to be noticed by others, we are making them our god. We are not seeking the reward and blessing of serving our God. In effect, we don't care if God notices or not, as long as people do. We feel good about ourselves if others notice us and are impressed. We rate our importance in terms of how impressed others are with us.

As with all hypocrisy, it looks good on the surface; even to ourselves. We learn, in Christian circles, to give the "right answers". We make sure we get to know the church leaders. We serve reliably, dependably, diligently. We look good—of course we do, since deep down that's the whole point of us serving in church. And then one day, the pastor asks you if you'd consider preaching next month; or becoming an elder or deacon; or speaking to a midweek group about Christian service. Inside your heart is bursting with pride as you humbly say that you'll pray about it.

There are a couple of easy ways to work out if this is why you serve. Think of a way you serve—it could be at church, or at home, and/or at work—and then ask yourself: *Would I do this thing if I knew that no one, other than me and God, would ever know I'd done it?* Or, right now, cast your mind back to the last time you served someone knowing that no one else would ever know what you'd done. If you can't remember that time—or you know that you cut corners to get it done quickly—then maybe this is you.

This attitude turns Christian service into competition. And that often makes us miserable—we look at friends and see that they are better servants than us, and we are crushed by it. It cuts away our identity. It means we won't be noticed, won't be known as impressive. We either give up "serving", or we serve more and more—but only to get our identity, our impressiveness, back.

If it doesn't make us miserable, this attitude makes us proud. This is something I know I do—I gloat. I compare myself to others, and I find myself better than them. This is because I am. I am totally serious. I am a better Christian than the friends I compare myself with. I have managed to make myself better than my friends by doing two things:

First, I lie to myself about myself.

This is a crucial strategy. I look at my strong points, and never at those of my friends. And I lie about my weaknesses. I generally find that when I sin it is someone else's fault, or that I am tired, or that life has been hard recently. It is amazing how regularly I am a victim, and how easily understandable my sin is. To be honest, when you take out all the sin in my life that is because of tiredness, there is hardly any left. The Bible tells me I'm not perfect, but I must be pretty close.

And then second, I drag other Christians down in my mind.

When I hear someone else preaching, I look for the mistakes. I have a running commentary in my head about how I would have preached that passage better than him. Or I look for my friend's sin, and turn it over in my mind and enjoy it. Which is strange, isn't it? It's strange that I think like this when I say I follow a God who delights to cover over His friends' sin, rather than delighting to notice, expose and enjoy it.

Serving... to belong

I remember the guy picked to be the head boy of my school. He was a straight-A student, captained the cricket team and played for the first team in rugby. He was picked first for playground football, and first by the girls. He was also a really good bloke.

I wasn't anything like him! Hardly ever picked (the "last pick" isn't actually picked at all—they just have to have you on the team!). I wanted to be "in", to be chosen, to be included in the team, the gang, the party.

People want to belong. We want to know that we are in the inner circle. We fear that there is a better party going on and we've not even been told about it, let alone invited. We want to have the easy confidence that I saw in our head boy at school.

I think it is this desire to join the in-crowd that made one particular guy behave so oddly when the gospel message reached Samaria, an area north of Jerusalem, shortly after Christ had risen and returned to heaven. Simon "practised sorcery ... and amazed all the people of Samaria" (Acts 8 v 9). When the evangelist, Philip, turned up, those people turned to Christ, as did Simon (v 12-13). Shortly afterwards, Peter and John came to the same area.

> When they arrived, they prayed for [the Samaritan converts] that they might receive the Holy Spirit, because the Holy Spirit had not yet come upon any of them ... Then Peter and John placed their hands on them, and they received the Holy Spirit.

When Simon saw that the Spirit was given at the laying on of the apostles' hands, he offered them money and said, "Give me also this ability so that everyone on whom I lay my hands may receive the Holy Spirit."

Peter answered: "May your money perish with you, because you thought you could buy the gift of God with money! You have no part or share in this ministry, because your heart is not right before God. Repent of this wickedness and pray to the Lord. Perhaps he will forgive you for having such a thought in your heart. For I see that you are full of bitterness and captive to sin."   (Acts 8 v 15-23)

Why did Simon want to buy the Holy Spirit? Because he wanted to do what the apostles could do, to be like them. Peter saw right through him when he talked about having a "part or share in this ministry". In Simon's eyes, the apostles were a powerful in-crowd, and he wanted in.

You get it at work, in clubs, in schools (staffrooms as well as playgrounds), sometimes in families... and almost always in churches. There is a perceived inner circle, a clique, a group that matters. These people may not have offices or titles, but their opinion counts for more. You might not be like me—not everyone is—but I am desperate to belong to this group, just once in my life. I serve to be like them, to be welcomed by them. I don't want to know the bitterness of being left on the periphery again. So I serve, and serve hard; and all my service is driven by my elevation of others to the status of my god:

To be good enough for Him
To get something from Him
To pay Him back

SERVING...

GOD

SERVING...
To impress
To belong

OTHERS

A wrong view of myself

Serving… because Jesus needs me

You get together with a couple of friends to catch up. As Becky says "hi" to Kate, you hear her thanking her for the flowers, help and encouragement when she heard she had lost her job. You immediately feel jealous and wonder why Becky didn't come to you for help, or why you weren't quicker off the mark when you heard her bad news.

If you feel jealous in situations like this, it could be that you serve to be needed. You need other people to need you. You want to be the one people turn to. This isn't ~~because you seek~~ their praise, or want others to know, it is because you need to matter, and you know you matter ~~because people can depend~~ on you. You matter because Jesus needs you. He needs you if He is to get His work done on earth now, in your church, in your family, in your community.

Maybe you are a bit like Martha, a woman to whose house Jesus came to stay:

> As Jesus and his disciples were on their way, he came to a village where a woman named Martha opened her home to him. She had a sister called Mary, who sat at the Lord's feet listening to what he said. But Martha was distracted by all the preparations that had to be made. She came to him and asked, "Lord, don't you care that my sister has left me to do the work by myself? Tell her to help me!"
> "Martha, Martha," the Lord answered, "you are worried and upset about many things, but only one thing is needed. Mary has chosen what is better, and it will not be taken away from her."
> (Luke 10 v 38-42)

What does Jesus need? He needs Martha to make all the preparations, doesn't He? If Martha doesn't work hard, things will fall apart, won't they? Martha is the Rock—the Lord Jesus is just a guy sitting in her front room. *No*, says Jesus—He doesn't need anything from Martha, and she only needs one thing. And she's missing out on it.

One way of spotting whether you have this perspective is that you're people-focused, but never God-centred. Notice what Martha *didn't* have time to do: she never sat down with her sister to spend time with Jesus. Of course not; she was too busy serving

Him! If you ever find yourself not listening to Jesus' words in Scripture because you feel there is too much "Christian service" to be done, might it be because you think He needs your work more than you need His words?

I want to pause here, because often the reason we work ourselves into the ground is because we don't want to let others down—which is commendable. We don't want others to be put out, or miss out, or (worse) drop out of the faith, when we could have done something—which is a right impulse. Because no one else will take that person out for a coffee and offer a shoulder to cry on so they will find comfort, will they? No one else will stay up till midnight cutting out star-shaped memory verses so that the children on Sunday will remember the Bible truths, will they?

Well, no; but also, yes. Jesus won't buy anyone a coffee, or cut out those stars. But He doesn't *need* you to comfort someone. He doesn't *need* you to plant truths in children's hearts. He's quite capable of doing those things without you. He may do those things through you; but He doesn't depend on you, and He never asks your service to be at the expense of your faith, rest or joy.

You and I are no one's saviour, no one's ultimate refuge or rock. Jesus has done and is doing far more for His people than we ever can or will. This is part of Christian freedom; we're free not to feel ultimately responsible; free to trust Jesus to comfort, to teach and to keep His people. We're liberated by knowing there is a Saviour, Refuge, Rock; and that it's not us. We are free to say: *Enough.*

How can we know if, for whatever reason, we are living as though the Lord needs us to serve? Simply ask: *What if?* about your service. *What if I stopped doing the children's ministry? What if I didn't visit that person every week? What if I didn't record the sermon? What if I didn't play guitar?* Do you believe, really believe, that Jesus would still achieve His purposes for your church? Or, deep down, do you think things would fall apart... that you are absolutely indispensable... that Jesus does, in actual fact, need your service? Towards the end of this chapter, I'll suggest the possibility of giving up an area of service. If you think that's just totally unrealistic for you, does that perhaps reveal that you believe that Jesus needs you?

Serving... but I don't need Jesus

"The youth group will be here in ten minutes. Food's ready, chairs are out, room's tidy. I've prepped the Bible study. Maybe I should pray. Oh, hang on, I was going to organise a really good game which will really help the teenagers to re-member the message. I can get that sorted in ten minutes, just about. Where did I put those toilet paper rolls, the shaving foam and the twelve rolls of tape..."

In the last chapter, we looked at serving in order to try to be good enough for God, to try to earn His acceptance. There is another type of service that is totally different, and totally similar. It is totally different because people who serve for this reason know that they are saved. They do not doubt that they are Christ's. There is no fear in their service.

But the similarity is that as they serve, there is no God; no dependence on Christ (I say "they"—often, this is "me"). Serving so God will love you has to be self-reliant—I am seeking to impress God with my work. But here is a sort of service that is just as self-reliant. It is the service of the competent Christian, who is busy and able... and too busy to pray, too able to need to beg Jesus for help.

If this is you, you're in good company. Jesus' first followers were like this. Mark's Gospel tells us of a man whose son is possessed by an evil spirit, making the boy's life a misery. He meets Jesus' disciples, and they get to work throwing the spirit out. They try everything, but it doesn't work. Along comes Jesus, who talks with the man, encourages him, and throws the demon out of his son. Later, the disciples ask their Lord:

> "Why couldn't we drive it out?" He replied, "This kind can come out only by prayer." (Mark 9 v 28-29)

They had used all their gifts, skills and efforts; but they hadn't done the only thing that would work. *They hadn't asked God.* They hadn't prayed. So everything else they did was a complete waste of time. Their attitude was self-reliant; they forgot to pray.

Have Christ's disciples changed much in the 2,000 years since then?! I wonder if this is the most-excused flawed service of all. We're quick to correct someone who serves to make God accept them, or to be noticed. But we smile understandingly when someone says they're not managing to have a "quiet time" at the moment; and we hold up as models men and women who work long and hard for Christ, without thinking about whether they pray long and dependently.

The famous eighteenth-century preacher, John Wesley, used to pray for two hours a day. A century ago, the pastor CH Spurgeon took four hours a day to speak to his Lord. These men also achieved a huge deal. But these were unusual, exceptional people. For most of us, we can neither pray like that nor achieve what they did. But if we had to choose one, we'd choose the achieving. And we do. I choose to *do* rather than *pray*. I often open my laptop and get to work before I close my eyes to speak to God. Like the disciples with that man and his son, I often try to help a friend, but never get round to praying for him.

Do you need Jesus? Do you pray before you serve? If something had to give, which would it be?

Giving up

We have seen the roots of skewed service of Jesus:

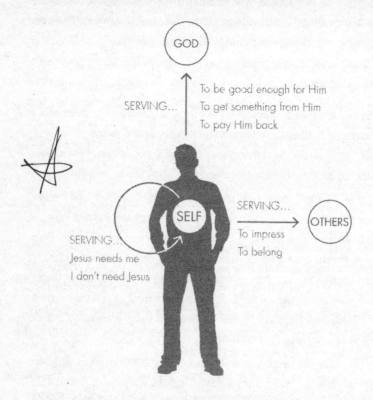

They are each different, and we struggle with different ones, in different ways, at different times. But there is one thing that unites them all. When we serve for any of these reasons, *we will give up*. These motivations for service are limited. They all lead to the same place: the dull drudgery of cheerless duty. They lead us to be bitter with God; annoyed with others; desperately disappointed with ourselves.

And when we reach that place, we are not far off giving up on loving Jesus.

So we give up, even while we keep on going. It looks like this: The pastor walks up to 24-year-old Jim, and asks him to take on running the sound system at church. Jim loves Jesus and is bowled over with gratitude to Him, so eagerly says yes. Over the years, the church grows, and so does the job. A decade later, Jim is there early for every service and is one of the last to leave. No-one ever thanks him, least of all Jesus. The wife Jim has prayed for never arrived. Neither did the children. Or the new job. Jim can't really recall why he said yes in the first place. But at least, for a while, it has felt as if the Sunday serving has balanced out the previous week's sins and made him feel better, though that feeling has now started to fade.

Jim can vaguely remember that when he started overseeing the sound system, he loved Jesus much more. And he loved serving Jesus much more, too. These days, it's only as he drives home from church that he feels lighter, with the rest of the day to enjoy. He's forgotten that he used to enjoy driving *to* church.

In his heart, Jim is giving up on Jesus. But a sense of duty, habit and gentle pressure from the pastor keeps him serving. After all, if he didn't do it, who would?

In Jim's heart, Christ Jesus is not a good God; He is a distant taskmaster. Faith is choking to death under the weight of service. This is what it feels like to be motivated in our service by a wrong view of God, of others, and of ourselves.

Give up!

Jim is not a real person. He is a whole lot of real people.

If you can see some of Jim in you, then it is well worth thinking hard about whether you need to give up serving in that way. It would be better to give up serving now than to give up serving in a year because you've given up on Jesus. Remember, Jesus doesn't love you because you work hard. And He doesn't need you to work hard—He managed without you on the coffee or stewarding teams of your church from the creation of the cosmos till a few years ago. If you're sat reading and the thought keeps coming: *I know this is me. But I can't stop for a while to sort my heart out. I'm the only cleaner. I'm the one who lives close enough to open up. I'm the pastor* then remember: it is better to quit your job than to lose your Lord.

You might not be able to do this overnight. It might be complicated to extricate yourself from areas of service, particularly if it is your job. But think and pray about it, and do this with other Christians and work out if there are things you need to give up so that you don't give Jesus up.

Now it's time to stop looking at ourselves so much, and fix our eyes on Jesus. He did not come to make us wallow in the misery of our sin, but to free us from it. So do read on. But in case you haven't got time to now, here's something to think about. Whatever you have seen in yourself that makes you sad and downcast, God in heaven saw it first. And it did not stop Him sending His Son to get you. He loved you when He first saw your sin, and He loves you now.

The amazing thing is not so much that we sin as we do, but that our Father loves us like He does. The amazing thing is that God wants us to look away from our flawed service, and to look at someone else's flawless service.

Christianity, it turns out, has nothing to do with our service at all.

5. Served by Christ

I don't like looking in the mirror very much. I particularly don't like looking close-up in the mirror! And in writing the last two chapters, I didn't really like looking at my own heart, and all those flawed reasons I serve. I'm guessing you didn't much enjoy it, either.

So we're going to stop. Stop looking at ourselves and turn somewhere a whole lot better. The counter-intuitive truth I've come to realise—the truth that prompted me to write this book—is that the only way to get our service of Jesus right is to realise that supremely, we don't serve Him. He serves us. The way to serve without sinking is to get to grips with the strange reality that Christians are not servants; they are served.

It's a truth that, once you're looking for it, runs throughout the Bible. We're going to focus on it, though, in just one verse. It's a familiar verse to many Christians. It's a famous verse, a verse I heard hundreds of times before the Spirit pointed out the dynamite in it. Here it is—Jesus told His followers:

> For even the Son of Man did not come to be served, but to
> serve, and to give his life as a ransom for many.
>
> (Mark 10 v 45)

Let's get into it straight away.

For even the Son of Man….

This is a sentence about someone who came to serve. This someone is "the Son of Man". He is clearly important—the way Jesus says "even" indicates this is not someone you would expect to serve. So who is he?

The phrase "son of man" first crops up in the Bible in Numbers 23 v 19, where it simply means "human". *So far, so ordinary!* But as the Bible story unfolds, it comes to mean far more than that. In the book of Ezekiel, it is the title that the Lord uses to refer to Ezekiel, His prophet.

During his life, Ezekiel has some amazing visions and meetings with God, but this is not where the stress falls. It falls rather on what God says to him after he sees the visions. After his first vision, he "heard the voice of one speaking" (Ezekiel 1 v 28). He hears the voice of the LORD speaking to him, and that voice calls him "son of man". At that moment, Ezekiel is filled with the Spirit, and is raised to his feet. The voice then continues:

> Son of man, I am sending you to the Israelites, to a rebellious nation ... And whether they listen or fail to listen ... they will know that a prophet has been among them.   (Ezekiel 2 v 3-5)

The son of man is the Spirit-filled prophet who sees the LORD God, hears His voice and passes on the message to His people. The son of man is not merely a man; he is God's man, sent to God's people. *He is no ordinary man.*

The trajectory of the title "son of man" continues in the book of the prophet Daniel:

> In my vision at night I looked, and there before me was
> one like a son of man, coming with the clouds of heaven.
> He approached the Ancient of Days and was led into his

presence. He was given authority, glory and sovereign power; all peoples, nations and men of every language worshipped him. His dominion is an everlasting dominion that will not pass away, and his kingdom is one that will never be destroyed.   (Daniel 7 v 13-14)

Here, the son of man is the Lord Himself, the second person in the family of God known as the Trinity. The Lord God who was, indeed, born as a man, Jesus of Nazareth. So by the time Jesus uses it of Himself in the Gospel of Mark, "Son of Man" means the Spirit-filled man who is God, who comes to speak the word of God to His people and to establish His kingdom.

There is no other man who compares to this Man in authority, glory, splendour or power. The glory, pomp and majesty of the Diamond Jubilee celebrations for Queen Elizabeth II reflected her authority and glory, and (if you like that kind of thing) were hugely impressive. But they were nothing compared to the day of this King, this Son of Man. She is only one of many earthly monarchs, ruling over an empire that has shrunk greatly since her reign began. He is the King of kings and rules over the cosmos. His day will be one where every knee bows to His glory and majesty. *He is a uniquely extraordinary Man.*

And this Son of Man...

...Did not come to be served...

Imagine it's the 100 metres final at the 2012 Olympic Games. Lord Coe, the man in charge of the Games, comes to take his seat. He walks past the crowds of people waiting outside, straight to the best seat in the stadium. Someone brings him a drink and something delicious to eat. He settles down to watch the greatest race from the greatest vantage point.

But, just before the gun goes, a steward mentions to him that a loo has broken in toilet block 174. Lord Coe leaps up, whips out a wrench and heads over there to fix the plumbing. He misses the race, gets filthy and wet, but fixes the leak.

That never happened. Of course not. But that's a tiny flavour of what is going on here:

For even the Son of Man did not come to be served...

The Gospels in the Bible are the story of what happened when the uniquely powerful and majestic Son of Man came to live in His world. The Son of Man comes to His subjects... and He does not expect to be served! This is bizarrely different to what we expect from such a mighty King. He is God! He is the One who made all things. He is the One who is in charge of everyone and everything. He could rightly expect us to serve Him.

If the Lord God came and lifted the roof from the room you are in now, tearing back the clouds to show you His majesty and glory on His heavenly throne, you would fall on your knees. You would bow before His glory, and you would be expecting to do as He said.

Well, God did come. He came and walked in the lanes of Galilee. He ate and drank and chatted and hung out with people. Surely this was to test them out? There is a slogan I've seen on people's desks and screen savers which says: *The boss is coming, look busy.* I've seen a version that says: *Jesus is coming, look busy.* Which makes sense—if God is in the room, then He's not the one putting the kettle on or pouring the milk, is He?! He's the One being waited on, isn't He?

No, says Jesus, the Son of Man. *I did not come to be served.*

He chose the fisherman Peter to be His follower, but it wasn't because He needed Peter's fish. He chose Matthew the tax collector, but not because He wanted His accounts done. When a rich, young man wanted to follow Him, Jesus didn't flatter him in order to get funding for His mission—He let the man walk away. When the respected and influential religious teacher Nicodemus came to see Him, Jesus didn't try to convince him to endorse His approach to ministry.

Jesus didn't come for any of them to serve Him. And He didn't come to you for you to serve Him. Jesus says *Follow me* to us today, just as He did to Peter and Matthew when He walked on earth. But He is *not* saying: *Follow me so that you can serve me—after all, I'm the eternal, all-powerful Son of Man. Now, let me tell you what to do.*

He *is* saying something almost impossible to believe.

...But to serve...

Jesus is saying: *Follow me and I will serve you.* Or, in His actual words:

> For even the Son of Man did not come to be served, but to serve.

He did not come so that you would serve Him. He came to serve you. Christianity is about Jesus, the God who serves His people.

Jesus comes into our lives to serve us. There is no catch, no small-print, no strings attached—there is just loving, humble, kind service by the Creator of the cosmos for His creatures, for us. Jesus' greatness is not that He can command the service of millions; it is that He serves millions.

If you follow Jesus, then your relationship with Him, your status before God the Father, and your having His Spirit with you, will never depend on how you serve Him. It is all about His service of you.

...And to give his life as a ransom for many

On 17 September 1992, a US F-111 fighter-bomber was returning to its base in the village of Upper Heyford, Oxfordshire, England. The pilot, Captain Jerry Lindh, and navigator, Major David "Mike" McGuire, had been on a routine training flight. As they approached the runway, their aircraft suffered a total hydraulics failure, leaving the pilot with very little control of the plane.

The control centre at the base instructed the crew to eject. But ejecting would mean that the plane would crash into houses in the village. Captain Lindh and Major McGuire chose to stay at the controls and steer their damaged plane over the village. They just managed to clear all the houses.

But by this point, it was too late for them to eject. They were both killed in the crash. No one else was injured.

How do you respond to such bravery? I find it hugely moving. These men didn't know the people in the houses, and it wasn't their fault that the plane had broken. Yet they chose to die to save the lives of others. It is amazingly impressive. And it is God-like. Astonishing though their actions were, they are mere reflections of what Jesus did for us. He came:

> ...to serve, and to give his life as a ransom for many.

Who are the "many"? People, like you and me. We all need ransoming, rescuing. All humanity, from Adam our first father, have turned away from the Lord. We have a God who is Lord of all, and yet chooses to be a servant. We, on the other hand, are servants who like to think we are lords. We love to rule; we love to lord it over each other. We love to gain respect, obedience, even fear.

This is just one way we have turned our backs on God. We may not feel that we have wronged God, but He has given us everything we have, and our lives so rarely show that. My life is about John, not Jesus. If I treated my parents with as little love, concern, time or gratitude that I show to my God, you would feel sorry for them and angry towards me. But that's how we all treat God—and often without even noticing, far less caring.

Jesus says: "Greater love has no-one than this, that he lay down his life for his friends" (John 15 v 13). We may well agree. But we did not deserve to be counted His friends. "God demonstrates his own love for us in this: While we were still sinners, Christ died for us" (Romans 5 v 8) . Jesus served us by dying for us. We were sinners and He died for us. We were His subjects, and He subjected Himself to death for us.

It is an amazing thing to die for anyone, but to die for your enemies is generosity that is hard to grasp. Think back to those airmen. They didn't know the people in the houses, yet they steered away from them to their own deaths. But imagine that in fact they had known the inhabitants down below. That they had known that one resident had bullied the pilot's son; that another had broken the navigator's daughter's heart; that another had burgled one of their mothers. Now imagine they chose to die instead of them.

Jesus knows us. Knows the thoughts we're glad others don't... knows the secrets we keep well hidden... knows how we've treated others, and treated Him. And He chose to die for us, out of love for us, despite all that.

It gets even harder to grasp when we see *why* He had to die for us. He gave his life "as a ransom". He had to pay a price to rescue us, and that price was His life.

This is because we had all cut ourselves off from God. When we turn our backs on God, we turn our backs on the source of life itself. To reject God is to reject life. Jesus' judgment on this is chillingly fitting. Those who reject Him will live without Him. He will shut them "outside" his eternal kingdom, in the "darkness" (Matthew 8 v 12). This is hell: being cut off from God's life and love. It is a conscious death.

Jesus loves us enough to come and warn us about hell; and He loves us enough to come and rescue us from hell. He has paid a ransom to buy us out of this terrible situation. He gave His life, executed on a wooden cross outside the city of Jerusalem. As He died, the sky went dark, and He cried out that His Father had turned His back on Him. Jesus went through hell. He went through the hell of being cut off from God His Father, the source of life and love.

He died the death we deserve. That was the ransom. There is nothing more terrible and wonderful in all of history than the day when the unique and glorious Son of Man displayed the glory of His love for us by dying our death, enduring our hell, paying our ransom.

This is how Jesus Christ serves you. It is amazing. But familiarity can breed contempt, or complacency. So if you've known this for years, or decades, why not pause here to appreciate the depth of this loving service. There is nothing else, can never be anything else, like it.

He died for you.

Being Mary

The Bible often shows us a tension between what humans expect and what we need. We expect that we must serve God for Him to love and accept and bless us. In fact, we need to know the loving Son of Man, who came to serve us, to accept and bless us.

We saw the two attitudes side-by-side in the same house when we looked at Martha and her sister in the last chapter. Martha, you'll remember, was...

> distracted by all the preparations that had to be made. She came to him and asked, "Lord, don't you care that my sister has left me to do the work by myself? Tell her to help me!"
>
> (Luke 10 v 40-41)

I really feel for Martha here! Wouldn't you rush around if Jesus turned up at your home? I would be running down to the shops, trying to clean the bathroom without Him noticing, dusting off my Bible, and so on.

It's understandable that Martha races around. The Son of Man has come to her home, and she's reacting in a totally right way, it seems. Mary, on the other hand, is surely being lazy and thoughtless. She's letting her sister do it all. She'll eat the feast, having sat still while Martha sweated.

Our lives regularly feel like Martha's. We are worried and upset about many things. Being a Christian just feels like an addition to the number of things to do!

So we can understand why she is pretty cross with her sister. It's not her complaint, but Jesus' reply, that is staggering. It just doesn't feel right:

> Martha, Martha ... you are worried and upset about many things, but only one thing is needed. Mary has chosen what is better, and it will not be taken away from her.
>
> (Luke 10 v 41-42)

To follow Jesus is not about serving Him. It is not about doing anything for Him. It is about sitting at His feet and listening to Him, the One who has done all we need. It is about being a Mary, not a Martha.

Jesus doesn't want servants, He wants friends. Jesus did not come to help us learn how to be worthy servants—He came to die because we are not worthy servants.

> For even the Son of Man did not come to be served, but to
> serve and to give his life as a ransom for many.

Why would you *not* follow this God? Why would you *not* sit at His feet for the rest of your eternal life?

It may be that, as you read the last couple of chapters, you've realised that you don't really know and enjoy the assurance of Jesus' love, and acceptance, and blessing. You've worked for it... perhaps you've been going to church for decades... but you've never had it. Or you haven't had it for years. Forget about your service. Look at His. He gave His life for you, to give you life with Him. Come to Him!

Or perhaps you feel burdened, weighed down, embittered or puffed up by church commitments. If Sunday provokes dread, or annoyance, or pride, or weariness, come to Jesus. He doesn't call you to come and serve Him. He calls you to see that He came to serve you.

It's only if we see that, first and foremost, we are not servants, we are served, that we can know the joyful freedom of the Christian life. And as we do that, we'll find that we serve like we never served before. Not serving as servants, though—because through coming to Jesus the Servant God, we now have a completely different identity.

6. Friends with the Boss

We are used to having loads of Facebook friends, work friends, family friends. We use the word "friends" quite lightly. We measure friends in quantity rather than quality, and not just on social media sites. Yet at the same time we all have, or long for, friends who are closer than this. Friends we can really trust; who will have our backs, no matter what.

This echoes the view of friendship that Jesus has:

> Greater love has no-one than this, that he lay down his life for his friends. You are my friends if you do what I command. I no longer call you servants, because a servant does not know his master's business. Instead, I have called you friends, for everything that I learned from my Father I have made known to you. (John 15 v 13-15)

Jesus defines a friend of His as someone He would die for. And so He no longer calls His disciples "servants" any more, because they are His friends. If you're a Christian, Jesus died for you. That's the kind of friend He sees you as.

Over the next three chapters, we're going to look at what Christ ransomed us for; or more accurately, who Christ ransomed us to be. And first, He died to make us His friends.

Friends Jesus dies for

I recently read an account of a group of soldiers in Afghanistan who were trapped in the middle of a minefield they had stumbled into. Several were injured, and the medic showed incredible bravery in moving around between them to treat them as they waited for a helicopter to evacuate them. Each move could have killed him; still he attended to the wounded.

Soldiers risk their lives each day of active duty. They do it for their country; but usually, if you ask one of them why they risk their lives, they'll tell you it's for the other men in their patrol. It's for their friends.

Jesus applies that kind of standard of friendship to His relationship with His followers. He risks His life... He *gives* His life... for us.

When Jesus says that His disciples are not merely servants, but friends, it's no throwaway line to make us feel nice. It means something; and it helps reshape our motives for serving Jesus. Take the idea of serving to impress others. If I have a view of Jesus as being my fairly distant boss, then I may well serve to impress Him or to impress the middle-management in His company (my pastor, Bible-study leader and so on).

Jesus declaring me to be His friend cuts this away. A good friendship is not based on impressing each other! Since Jesus is our Friend, He wants us to be friends with each other—to "love one another" in the way He loves us (John 15 v 17). If I remember that Jesus is my Friend, and that my Bible-study leader is my friend, then I won't keep trying to impress them. I don't need to. I'll be free to get on with enjoying knowing them.

Friends Jesus shares with

When I book a taxi to the station, I expect that I'll get in, confirm where I'm going, and then the driver will take me there. I don't expect the driver to ask me if I really need to go to the station, to check if I know what time the train is, or to make sure I definitely want to travel today. I am paying the driver to take me there—he doesn't need to know why!

A servant does as he is told. He doesn't understand what his master's plan is, or need to know the big picture. He has no right to ask or receive an answer. He "does not know his master's business" (v 15). It is enough for him to understand what he must do, and get on with it.

But you and I are not just servants. We are friends with the Boss. He does tell us what He's up to, and why. We know His business, which changes the way we work for Him.

At some point in your Christian life, you may have been told something like: *You don't need to know why—it is enough that God said you should do it.* Or that something is wrong *because the Bible says it is wrong.* There is some truth in these, but also a massive mistake. The implication is that God is unknowable—He is a bit odd, perhaps arbitrary, certainly incomprehensible. We should do what we're told and not expect God to tell us why.

During the Crimean War in the 1850s, a British cavalry formation called the Light Brigade were ordered to charge straight at some Russian cannon. Alfred Tennyson's poem, *The Charge of the Light Brigade*, contains some famous lines:

> Theirs not to make reply,
> Theirs not to reason why.
> Theirs but to do and die:
> Into the valley of Death
> Rode the six hundred.

The tone of a lot of Christian encouragement to serve God is similar to this. Off we trot into the valley of Death (or, at least, the vale of difficult and tiring service), like some spiritual Light Brigade. It is the death of any closeness with God—because if we are simply to obey Him without question, then we are merely servants. Servants can't expect to be close to their master; they can't expect ever to have things explained to them. Just obey; let God figure out the why; it's above your pay-grade!

But Christ says:

> I no longer call you servants, because a servant does not
> know his master's business. Instead, I have called you
> friends, for everything that I learned from my Father I have
> made known to you.

Jesus has taken the secret things that belonged to the Lord and shared them with His disciples. He has shared "everything that I learned from my Father". So the twelve disciples of Jesus were His friends, because He told them everything. He then made sure they wrote it down, and gave them His Spirit so that they wrote it down right. So we too know everything! We can open the Bible and we see everything, from how Jesus made the world right through to how He will remake it on the day of judgment.

Christ didn't choose a few special people and give them secret knowledge. He didn't appoint an inner circle of priests or ministers who have a special relationship with Him. He didn't make it difficult so that only an elite intellectual group could understand it. He didn't make it costly so that only the wealthy were welcomed. He made it simple, and He put it in a book, and He put that book into hundreds of languages, and He put it into millions of hands. He wanted everyone to know Him, to know His Father, to know their plans. He wants a lot of friends!

Knowing "everything"

This "everything" that Jesus tells us is what He learned from His Father. We tend to think of truth as correct facts. God's view of truth is a bit different. It is not less than correct facts, but it is much more. It is true relationships. Indeed, the "truth" is a person, not an idea (John 14 v 6).

This means that the "everything" we are told by Jesus in the Bible is not every fact about everything everywhere, but everything about relating to God.

If you are as old as me, you may remember the film *Highlander*. It is about a group of immortals who fight each other down the centuries with swords. They are competing for the "prize", which is all knowledge. The quest for this prize—to know everything—drives so much scientific work. It is something we long for. I'd love to know exactly what stars are made of, or what sorts of creatures live at the bottom of the ocean, or even why my computer doesn't know my printer exists when they are blatantly plugged into each other. But the knowledge we really cry out for is not so much scientific and factual, but rather emotional and relational. We would love to know why we are still single, or why the Lord healed one friend and let another die, or why we can't seem to get through to our children.

The knowledge that Jesus shares with His friends isn't the specific answers to all these questions. He may tell us why to some of these, but He may not. What he gives us is much better. He tells us that His Father is our Father. He makes it possible for His Father to be our Father. And He tells us His Father loves us and does what is best for us; loves us enough to rescue us and guide us and change us. He gives us a real, deep, true relationship with God as our Father. We know God. And we know Him as in control, and acting in love.

To a cynic, this sounds like a cop-out. But in real life, it matters more. As you sit there stunned while a senior doctor tells you that you have cancer, or your wife or your son does, it might be some comfort to know the exact "why". But far more necessary and wonderful is to know God; and to know that He is in control, and that He is good. We do not merely *know about* God; we *know* God.

When a child falls and grazes her knee and runs to her mother, she doesn't want an explanation about why skin gets cut when it scrapes the ground. She doesn't want to have it explained that she needs to slow down more for corners. She wants a hug. The desire for answers is an expression of our desire to know that there is a loving purpose in all things. It is a desire to know God. It is a desire for Him. That is truth—true love more than true facts.

This is what makes the difference when we don't understand what God is doing. We are not in the position of those Light Brigade horsemen ordered to their deaths—simply bound by duty to obey commands we don't understand. We are not even in the position of servants, obeying a God we trust to give good orders when we don't understand. We are friends.

Jesus has explained to us what He is doing. He often even shows us the details. When He doesn't, or we don't understand, we don't have to fall back on knowing that He is morally good, like we might know that a headteacher is morally good. We can fall back on His friendship. We can trust Him to be more than good, to be good *to us*, to be at work *for us*. We can trust Him to explain it to us later; trust Him as a friend who has our backs, not simply as a boss who makes good calls.

Friends who share Jesus

This friendship has big implications. It means that if we think of ourselves as servants but not as friends, then we will end up giving the wrong impression of Christ.

Imagine you are chatting to a non-believing friend over a coffee. She says she's heard that Christians give a big chunk of their income to church, sort of like a tax. *Is this true?* she asks. *Why would you do that?*

If you answer that the Bible says that Christians should indeed give a proportion of their income to church, and so you do just that, then you have been a good servant. You have explained your Master's decision, and you have shown that His word is enough for you—you will obey Him. You might even go further, and explain that you know your Master is a good God, so He must have a good reason for this.

In doing this, you have said what is true. But you have given the wrong impression of God. You have painted Him as a distant Master who you must obey. You have shown that Christians are those who trust God, but do not think He might explain His decisions. This is a tough pill for many in our culture to swallow, when we are often suspicious of power, and very wary of giving our trust to those who wield power in ways we don't understand. In this example, it makes God a bit like the taxman—probably a good thing, but if you can find a way to avoid Him...

Of course, you have good reason to trust Jesus and you can explain to your friend how He died for you and so is worthy of your blind trust. But blind trust is still a big ask for your friend. And the problem is that it is something Jesus doesn't ask of her. He doesn't ask for blind trust—He asks for eyes-wide-open trust.

Jesus has explained why it is a joy for us to give our money to further His kingdom. He has told us that it frees us from being slaves to money, from worshipping wealth, which will only disappoint (Colossians 3 v 5). He has told us God provides for our needs (Matthew 6 v 24-34). He has told us that we can use our money wisely to invest in His eternal kingdom, rather than treasures in this world that will rot in time (Matthew 6 v 19-21).

Now, the fact that Christ has shared everything with us in the book the Holy Spirit wrote about Him doesn't mean that we will always be able to answer every question. Or that we'll remember all He's said! But if you didn't know what to say to this friend who is asking about Christian financial giving, you could still give the right impression of Jesus. You don't have to simply say: "Jesus says so, so I have to do it".

Instead, you can answer that you don't know why Jesus says we should give money to the work of our church, but you know that He must have a good reason, because that's the kind of Boss and Friend He is to His people. What's more, you expect that He has put the answer in the Bible because He is your Friend, and He likes to explain things to you. You can say that you'll look at the Bible, pray, maybe chat with some Christian friends, and get back to her. Then you can talk about how you enjoy being able to trust Jesus when you don't understand, and how you enjoy the reality that He trusts you with His heart and His plans. You can talk about how you enjoy following the God who calls you His friend, and not just His servant.

None of this is to say that you and I are not servants. God is our Boss, our Lord. But you're not serving some giant corporation, with layers of middle-management and a boss who is hard-working and dedicated, but who you never see and can never know. You are working for your Friend.

A guy I know works for a small company, and his boss is also a friend. This guy works long hours. He often goes an extra mile to do something for his boss. Why? It's not for a pay rise, or because he has to, or even because the boss asks him to. It's because his boss is his friend.

Think of an area of Christian service you're involved in. Consider how you'll think about it, and do it, if you think of yourself as simply a servant.

Now consider the difference it will make if you remember you're doing it as a friend, as a friend to the One who gave His life for you, the One who has trusted you with knowing and being part of His plans.

When we serve as Jesus' friends, we find our serving changes. We don't serve because we have to or need to, but because we want to. We are His friends. He loves us. And the joy returns.

7. Bride of the King

I was friends with Flick for a long time before we were married. Before we started going out, we spent a lot of time telling people we were just good friends. This was true—though in our hearts, both of us were hoping for more. And our friends didn't buy it anyway—they had a sweep-stake on when we would get married!

I really enjoyed being "just friends" with Flick—but it is *so* much better to be married to her. And once we were husband and wife, it would have been a real shame if we'd kept acting as though we were merely good friends. We would have missed out on the physical intimacy of marriage. We would have missed out on enjoying the closeness and reassurance that comes from knowing that, no matter what, we have committed ourselves to each other until we die.

We've seen that Jesus has made us His friends, and that's amazing. But if that's as far as we get in our thinking about who we are as Christians, then we are missing out. Because Christ says we are His bride. You and I are married to Him.

Followers of Jesus, His church, are also His bride. Jesus is our Husband. If you've not come across this idea before, it might sound a bit strange (and if you have come across it, it might not sound that straightforward either!). It raises lots of questions. What does it mean for lots of people, the church, to make up just one person, the bride? How do we apply a romantic, sexual relationship to our relationship with Jesus? How do we enjoy closeness with a husband who we can't see at the moment?

These questions are good—but they come from starting with human marriages and then trying to work out how Jesus and His church's marriage maps onto our lifelong unions. The Bible says that really, it's the other way around:

> "For this reason a man will leave his father and mother and
> be united to his wife, and the two will become one flesh."
> This is a profound mystery—but I am talking about Christ
> and the church. However, each one of you also must love
> his wife as he loves himself, and the wife must respect her
> husband.   (Ephesians 5 v 31-33)

Paul is quoting from Genesis 2 v 24, where God makes the first human marriage, between Adam and Eve. But then he says that "I am talking" not about Adam and Eve, or John and Flick, but "about Christ and the church" (v 31-32). The most "profound mystery"—the foundational marriage, onto which we map all other marriages—is the one between Jesus and His people.

This means that we don't look at our marriages to learn things about Christ's—which tends to lead to some confusion and to us mentally filing these truths away under the heading *Important, but incomprehensible and a bit weird*. We need to look at the way Jesus and the church relate to one another and learn things about our marriages. I don't look at the way I love Flick and conclude that Jesus loves us like that. Instead, I need to look at the way Jesus loves us and conclude that I should love Flick like that (gulp!).

We are servants of Christ, but not merely servants, because we are friends. But we are not even simply friends—we are His bride.

It is the most beautiful of stories, and it resonates through all the good stories. One day a girl is scrubbing floors and scouring pots. Then a horse whinnies outside and the doorway is blocked by a tall, handsome man holding a perfectly-fitting glass slipper. The next day, Princess Cinderella wakes up in silk sheets next to her new husband (weddings are easier to organise in fairytales).

But this plotline isn't confined to a fairytale. It is the deepest truth the cosmos knows. It is true love. Prince Charming is a pale reflection of the Prince who left the loftiest palace to find a slave and make her into His bride. The truth is far more beautiful than the make-believe, because the Husband is far more wonderful.

Jesus loves His bride sacrificially

Prince Charming gave up his reputation to marry Cinderella. He would have given up any chance of a strategic marriage (not that such things are very important in the land of Far Far Away). Jesus gave up far more. Earlier in Ephesians 5, Paul tells married men:

> Husbands, love your wives, just as Christ loved the church
> and gave himself up for her.   (Ephesians 5 v 25)

How did Jesus give Himself up for His bride? And why? He gave Himself, supremely, when He gave His life. The greatest act of love in history was when the church's Husband died on a cross. But why did Jesus give Himself up? "For her". Not that He was making some silly, romantic gesture on the cross to "prove" how much He loves us. Jumping in front of a bus and getting hit to show your love is stupid. Jumping in front of a bus and getting hit to push your wife out of the way is love.

This is what verse 26 is getting at. Christ gave His life "to make her holy, cleansing her by the washing with water through the word". In His death, Jesus did two things for us. He gave us His perfection, His holiness—He made us perfect like Him. He gave us all He has. And He took our dirt, our sin, and died for them Himself. He took all we have.

In a marriage service, husband and wife commit to sharing all they have. In our case, Flick got my collection of action films, and I got her CD collection, allowing me for the first time to pass myself off as a man of culture and taste. In the same way, Jesus and His people share all they have. We give Him our sin, and He dealt with it and destroyed it on the cross. He gives us His holiness, and we enjoy being perfect in God's sight for ever.

This is how Jesus loves His people. This is the most wonderful marriage, and every time a husband gives up what's easiest for him to do what's best for his wife, it's a small glimpse of it.

Most men want to be worthy of the woman they love. We want to show that we can care for our bride, love her, protect her and provide for her. In stories and films, this can go to extreme lengths, with the woman watching the man prove his worthiness as he slays the dragon or takes down the bad guy. Of course, in our world it requires great guts simply for a man to meet his fiancée's parents. The knights and cowboys can probably be heard muttering about when men were men...

Jesus is the ultimately worthy Husband. He slew death and defeated the devil in order to take His bride up the aisle. Do you ever doubt that Jesus loves you, that He really does love *you*?

In reply, He simply points you to His cross. We are never left without this clear evidence of His love in His death. Whatever the situation you are in, and however you are feeling, the truth is that Jesus loves you. He died to make us His bride.

Jesus loves His undeserving bride

Now imagine if Prince Charming did something even stranger than marrying the lowly, but beautiful and lovely, Cinderella. Imagine he married the uglier of the two ugly sisters. Imagine he did this knowing exactly what she was like. Imagine he kept on loving her and being, erm, charming to her, even as she cheated on him with equally ugly men.

That would be no fairytale. You would never tell it to a child. But it was reality for one of God's prophets in the Old Testament, Hosea. God tells him to marry an unfaithful wife, Gomer. When he does, Gomer responds by continuing to sleep around, and has children with other men. She ends up selling herself into sex-slavery.

How is Hosea to respond? God tells him:

"Go, show your love to your wife again, though she is loved by another and is an adulteress. Love her as the LORD loves the Israelites, though they turn to other gods and love the sacred raisin cakes." So I bought her for fifteen shekels of silver and about a homer and a lethek of barley.

(Hosea 3 v 1-2)

Hosea is to love her again. He is to take her back. That means that he, the cheated husband, has to walk into her pimp's house, and pay his own money to buy her back. It means becoming a laughing-stock. It means being ashamed, abused, used and disgraced so that Gomer can be free, can live as his wife again. This is an almost unimaginably costly love.

Adultery is awful; that's what makes God's command to Hosea so shocking and provocative. And we should ask: *Why on earth would He ask something like this of His own prophet?* Because it's a picture. Hosea is going to "love her as the LORD loves the Israelites"; he'll love her in the way God loves His bride. The story of Hosea is the story of God and His people. When Paul talks about Jesus being the husband of the church in Ephesians 5, we need to keep Hosea and Gomer in mind.

And we are Gomer. We are not simply a poor Cinderella, a victim of our cruel sisters. No, the bride Jesus sacrifices Himself for is a whore. She is far worse than a prostitute. Many prostitutes have little choice or say in what they do. This wife, the church, has the greatest of husbands, but she turns away from Him and runs after other lovers. Throughout the Bible, the image of prostitution is used to describe the way God's people turn away from Him and worship other gods, love other things more than Him, serve them as though they are all they need.

We would expect the Lord to turn His back on us. We would expect Him to say: *Fine. You've made your bed—go and lie in it.* We would expect Him to walk away from us—after all, He has given us everything and we have walked away from Him.

Instead, He comes for us. The love of Hosea, amazing though it is, is nothing compared to the costly love of the God-Husband. Jesus had to pay the price of His own blood to buy us out of slavery. On the cross, that's what He did. And we will never appreciate the depth and wonder of the love of Christ unless we admit the depth and horror of our spiritual adultery. There's only one hero in the church's marriage to the Christ; and it's not the church.

Jesus loves His bride enough to change her

Jesus' love transforms His bride in two ways. The first is that it changes our status. On 29th April 2011, a lady called Catherine walked into a church as plain Miss Middleton. She walked out as a duchess! Her status was totally changed purely because of who she married—Prince William, Duke of Cambridge.

It is the same with us. The people of God are not mere servants. We have been given a beautiful white dress, and we walk on the arm of the King. We are a royal bride.

Appreciating this undoes the wrong motives we have for serving Jesus. When I cook a meal for Flick, I am enjoying serving her as an expression of my love. As I (slowly) chop the ingredients, I am enjoying being married to her. I am enjoying knowing the pleasure she will have not just from the meal, but from knowing that I lovingly cooked it. I am not cooking to get her to love me—she already does. Or to impress my friends—they'll never know, and that doesn't matter.

Again, it's worth pausing here, thinking of an area of Christian service you're involved in, and asking: *How would it transform my attitude if I remembered that I'm doing this for my Husband?*

But second, although we are a royal bride, we are still grubby. We are a long way from living out what it means to be the bride of Christ. So Jesus goes on transforming us; He goes on cleaning us. He marries us as we are, but He loves us too much to leave us that way. They say that men get married hoping their spouse will never change, and women get married desperately hoping theirs will! In this marriage, it's the opposite. We don't need our Husband to be anything more than He already is. He wants to make us into the beautiful bride we are not:

> Christ loved the church and gave himself up for her to make
> her holy, cleansing her by the washing with water through
> the word, and to present her to himself as a radiant church,
> without stain or wrinkle or any other blemish, but holy and
> blameless. (Ephesians 5 v 25-27)

Jesus will clean us up and get us ready for the day He comes back for us. It is not that He needs to clean us so He can love us. It is *because* He loves us so much that He will not leave us dirty. Our status is that of the holy and blameless bride of Christ. Our lives will match up to that one day.

Getting ready for our wedding

In most weddings, there's a party involving great food which follows the service where the couple actually get married. The service plus the feast equals the "wedding". But there is often a gap between the two, usually for vast numbers of photographs to be taken while guests stand around wondering when it will be time to eat!

It's helpful to realise that, though the church is Jesus' bride, we have not yet had the wedding feast. In a sense, the cross of Christ is the exchange of vows, where Jesus died to make us His bride. The return of Christ is the reception, the feast, and the beginning of fully enjoying married life. We're in the gap between the two.

What will the reception be like?

> Then I heard what sounded like a great multitude, like
> the roar of rushing waters and like loud peals of thunder,
> shouting: "Hallelujah! For our Lord God Almighty reigns. Let
> us rejoice and be glad and give him glory! For the wedding
> of the Lamb has come, and his bride has made herself ready.

Fine linen, bright and clean, was given her to wear." (Fine linen stands for the righteous acts of the saints.) Then the angel said to me, "Write: 'Blessed are those who are invited to the wedding supper of the Lamb!'" And he added, "These are the true words of God."   (Revelation 19 v 6-9)

There are lots of stories about how some women have planned their wedding days since they were three or four years old. I once heard a joke about a bride-to-be who booked the church and reception venue, chose her dress, selected her flowers, and practised throwing her bouquet... and then began to look for a man to marry!

Weddings matter. And our wedding day will be the day of our lives. Not the day Miss F. Harley became Mrs F. Hindley, but the wedding day when Jesus, the Lamb who died sacrificially for His bride, comes and sits with us at our wedding feast as our husband. Of course our wedding days in this world matter; of course we hope for wonderful, happy marriages in this life—but our wedding days and marriages are trailers for the main event, the ultimate wedding day, the greatest romance. It's what we should be looking to, planning for, dreaming of. It's why in the last few verses of the whole Bible we find that: "The Spirit and the bride say, 'Come!'" (Revelation 22 v 17).

And when He comes, Jesus will give us a beautiful wedding dress to wear: "Fine linen, bright and clean, was given her to wear. (Fine linen stands for the righteous acts of the saints)" (19 v 8).

The works of service that we do are not a way we impress Christ—they are His present to us. We will see more about this later on, but isn't that exciting? I have known a lot of friends and family who have got married. I have not yet met a bride who turned up in whatever clothes happened to be washed and ironed! Getting the right wedding dress is a huge investment in time, money, sweat and tears. (And frankly, whoever it was who decided that the husband-to-be couldn't see the dress till the day, so that he didn't have to be part of the sweat-and-tears stage, is someone I would like to buy a drink!) But it is also a huge delight to a bride—both the choosing and the wearing.

The righteous deeds of the saints—the good things we do in the service of Jesus—are a huge investment of our time, money, sweat and even sometimes tears. And they are meant to be a delight to us. They are our wedding dress. They are our glory. They are Jesus' gift to us, because He has broken with tradition and not only seen the dress, but made it Himself as beautifully as only the Creator of sunsets and stars can.

We're not serving Him as paid servants; we're serving Him as a wife, serving the Husband who loves her. Next time you're changing a nappy... or sweeping up after the prayer meeting... or preparing Sunday School... or trying to convince the pastor to turn his mic on so the sound works... you're serving and loving your wonderful Husband, and you're doing something which makes up your wedding dress. How will that affect how you feel as you serve?

See how much we lose if we think of ourselves primarily as servants? We don't eat downstairs—we feast with the King! He has come, and is coming, to marry us, and we can enjoy getting ready. We are His bride. He loves us.

8. Sons of the Father

A couple of months ago, I had one of my all-time favourite afternoons. I was sitting in the sun on our patio, building a flat-pack sandpit. I love making things, but I don't have much ability, so flat-pack is my level! As I was working on it, my two-year-old daughter, Daisy, woke up from her nap and came to help. She loves helping. She put screws in the holes (sometimes the right screws, and occasionally the right holes), lined up bits of wood, and generally got involved. She even found other bits of wood that she thought I might incorporate into the design.

It took a lot longer to build the sand-pit than I had anticipated. I had to move screws, help Daisy hold and use a screwdriver, and line up the wood several times over because Daisy liked to "adjust" it.

It took longer, but it was much more fun. Daisy had a great time, and so did I. I loved working with my child. It wasn't efficient, but we laughed a lot and enjoyed each other.

Now, line this sweet picture up with what Paul once told the people of Athens:

> The God who made the world and everything in it is the Lord
> of heaven and earth and does not live in temples built by
> hands. And he is not served by human hands, as if he needed

anything, because he himself gives all men life and breath
and everything else.   (Acts 17 v 24-25)

There are some beautiful temples around, but the Lord of
heaven and earth was not homeless before someone built Him
one. Lots of people do lots of things in service of God, but the
Sustainer of the universe is not powerless without them. God
does not need our service. So why does He have us work with
Him? Because of the relationship we have with Him. Because
we are His children.

Undeserving sons

Earlier on, we looked at Jesus' story about two sons. Let's look
more closely at what happened to the younger son after he took
his father's money and turned his back on his father:

> After he had spent everything, there was a severe famine in
> that whole country, and he began to be in need. So he went
> and hired himself out to a citizen of that country, who sent
> him to his fields to feed pigs. He longed to fill his stomach
> with the pods that the pigs were eating, but no-one gave him
> anything. When he came to his senses, he said, "How many
> of my father's hired men have food to spare, and here I am
> starving to death! I will set out and go back to my father and
> say to him: Father, I have sinned against heaven and against
> you. I am no longer worthy to be called your son; make me
> like one of your hired men."   (Luke 15 v 14-19)

Notice the speech that he prepares. He has realised that he
has acted terribly towards his father and cannot appeal to him
as a son any more. He has rejected his father and so has no
right to be treated as a son. Since he acted as though his father
were dead, he must think he is as good as dead to his dad. So

he simply hopes that there might be enough compassion in the father who he has so wronged to have him back as a servant. That's his hope.

He hopes in vain. There is no way this father will have his son back—as a servant.

> So he got up and went to his father. But while he was still a long way off, his father saw him and was filled with compassion for him; he ran to his son, threw his arms around him and kissed him.
> The son said to him, "Father, I have sinned against heaven and against you. I am no longer worthy to be called your son."
> But the father said to his servants, "Quick! Bring the best robe and put it on him. Put a ring on his finger and sandals on his feet. Bring the fattened calf and kill it. Let's have a feast and celebrate. For this son of mine was dead and is alive again; he was lost and is found." So they began to celebrate.
>
> (Luke 15 v 20-24)

There is no way this father will have him back as a servant. He will have him back as a son! The son doesn't even get to the end of his prepared apology. As soon as he gets to the part when he says he is no longer worthy to be called a son, his father interrupts. He immediately calls for the best robe—a son's robe, not a servant's. He puts a ring, a sign of love and authority, on his finger. He declares a feast for everyone. And he then utters words his son must have dreamed to hear, but knew he never could: "This son of mine".

We need to remember that the son is right! He doesn't deserve to be called this man's son. But the son doesn't decide if he gets to be a son, a servant, or nothing at all. That is the father's call. And he says: *You are my son.*

Hold that thought and look at Galatians 3 v 26-27:

> You are all sons of God through faith in Christ Jesus, for all
> of you who were baptised into Christ have clothed yourselves
> with Christ.

We are sons of God. *You* are a child of God! When we turn
back to God through faith in Christ Jesus, this is how our Father
welcomes us. We might expect that being the bride of Christ,
we would get to have God as our Father-in-law. Actually, the
marriage union that Jesus makes with us is much deeper than
any other marriage. We are so united to Jesus that we can be
considered one with Him. As Paul puts it here, we have clothed
ourselves with Christ.

Adopted sons

We are not called "sons" because there is something better
about men than women. The Bible calls us "children of God"
(Romans 8 v 21) and "sons and daughters" (2 Corinthians 6
v 18)—and, as we've seen, a "Bride". The reason why Christian
men and women are together often referred to as "sons" of God
is explained in Romans 8 v 15-17:

> For you did not receive a spirit that makes you a slave again
> to fear, but you received the Spirit of sonship. And by him we
> cry, "*Abba*, Father." The Spirit himself testifies with our spirit
> that we are God's children. Now if we are children, then we
> are heirs—heirs of God and co-heirs with Christ, if indeed
> we share in his sufferings in order that we may also share in
> his glory.

We are sons in the sense that we enjoy the same relationship
with God that Jesus does. In the Old Testament, which gives

the backdrop to this teaching, there is no difference between an adopted child and one born into the family (for example, Mordecai took Esther "as his own daughter when her father and mother died" in Esther 2 v 7). For us to be adopted by God as sons means that He sees and treats us in the same way as *the* Son. All that Jesus deserves, all that Jesus has, all His inheritance, all His glory, is shared with us. When God looks at you and me, He sees Jesus. He sees a son of His.

Sons in the family business

When the son came back to his father in Luke 15, he came back into the same relationship he had had before; but now he was in a position to enjoy it. Previously, he had thought he needed his father's stuff—now he sees that all he needs is his father's love.

The same love lies in the heart of God the Father for us as His sons. This is why we pray to God as Father. The Holy Spirit reminds us that we are sons, and so when we have needs, hopes and fears, He moves us to pray, to confide and cry out to our kind Father.

So what difference does all this make day by day? It becomes more natural to depend on Him; and it becomes more natural to work for Him, and to enjoy it. Surely that younger son would have whistled with glee as he walked into the fields the next day with his dad. The day before he'd woken up in a pigsty, hoping he might end it in a servants' dorm. Instead, he was a son! He would have swung his scythe into the corn with a smile of amazement that he could work alongside his dad as a son in the family business, not as a mere servant.

We get to work with our heavenly Father. Not because He needs our help (remember Daisy and me), but because He enjoys our company. He gives us the privilege of being part of what He is up to. He helps us and gives us the Holy Spirit and covers over our mistakes. He loves us working with Him because He loves us.

When you see it like this, then it keeps on changing how we serve God. How can I serve so that people will accept me, when I serve God as a son whose Father delights in him? How can I serve so that I belong, when I already belong in God's family? How can I serve to earn a blessing from God, when He has adopted me and made me heir to everything? How can I serve half-heartedly, or accept half-measures, when I'm a son in the family business?

This is the treasure of Christianity—not that we get to be good, not that we get heaven, not that we get blessing or joy or hope or peace. The treasure of Christianity is that we get *God*. We get to be with God as He works. We get to be part of how God works. We get God.

Daisy does not particularly enjoy carpentry. She does not particularly like wood and screws. She won't necessarily enjoy work as she grows up. But she enjoys being with me because I'm her father, and I enjoy being with her because I'm her father. The thought that God, with a love far purer and a joy far happier, delights in the same way to be with me, and you... that is some thought!

The God on the throne of heaven is a Father. He is *your* Father, Christian. We are not merely servants, simply friends, or even in-laws. We are His sons. He loves us.

9. Still being served

"Jesus died for us while we were still sinners. He's made me His friend, His bride, His brother. Wow! Now it's up to us, isn't it? Jesus is in heaven, but His mission down here continues. He's served me; now we need to serve Him. I serve Him by earning money to feed my family. And at church, too. After all, Jesus isn't going to get to church early and put the chairs out, is He?! Or make the tea? He's done His bit; now we do ours. Must go—I need to set up 50 chairs and get the urn on."

We are, above all, people who are served, not people who serve. And we've seen over the last few chapters that Jesus' service of us makes us His friends and bride, and His Father's children. We have begun to see how these amazing realities transform our service of Jesus. They undo the wrong motives we can have for service, by showing us that we have a much more happy and secure relationship with God and others than we sometimes think. Once we see this, the wrong motives for service lose their attraction.

But these great truths about who we have been ransomed to be also hint at something else. No good friend helps out a buddy once or twice, then puts his feet up. No good husband works hard to help and support his wife for the first few years of marriage, then lets her get on with it. No loving father waves goodbye to his son at 18, and locks the door behind him.

Christ's service of us happened in the past. But it is not only a past reality. He is serving us today just as surely as He did on Good Friday and Easter Sunday. He works from heaven now; but He is still working hard.

He is still serving us.

Jesus intercedes for us

> Because Jesus lives for ever, he has a permanent priesthood. Therefore he is able to save completely those who come to God through him, because he always lives to intercede for them. (Hebrews 7 v 24-25)

Jesus intercedes for us. This means two things. First, He is our representative before God the Father. Jesus stands in heaven a bit like our ambassador. An ambassador lives in a foreign capital city to represent his country to the government there. Jesus lives in the throne-room of God to represent His people before God His Father.

We do not deserve to come into the presence of God. But that is exactly what we can do. It is as though I am a street-cleaner in a nondescript English town who has a criminal record and a bad reputation, when suddenly I'm picked up by limo, flown to Washington DC on Air Force One, and ushered into the Oval Office of the White House, having been told by the US Ambassador to Britain: *The President wants to hear what you have to say.* Jesus brings us where we could never hope to go. We can be with, live with, and enjoy God as a Father.

The letter to the Hebrews shows us how this truth applies. It means that all Christians can always bring all their prayers and requests to God (4 v 16). We know that He will listen and answer, because Jesus stands there on our behalf. In Christ we have a perfect priest, the go-between we need who can bring together a sinful people and a holy God. Because Jesus intercedes for us, we don't pray to a distant deity, wondering if He cares about us, hoping to butter Him up so that He might give us what we want. We pray as children, who know that our Father loves us. He might not give us exactly what we ask for, but He will give us what we need.

Strangely, although Jesus interceding for us means we can pray, it also means that we don't have to. This is the second thing. To intercede is to plead on behalf of someone else. So Jesus prays for us, just as He did during His time on earth. The most beautiful example of this is in John 17. In this wonderful prayer for His followers, the Son asks the Father to "protect them" and "sanctify them" (v 11, 17). He tells His Father that "I want those you have given me to be with me where I am, and to see my glory" (v 24). And He says that this prayer is not only for the disciples who are in the room with Him as He speaks—"I pray also for those who will believe in me through their message" (v 20).

This amazing prayer finishes with Jesus saying:

> Righteous Father, though the world does not know you, I know you, and they know that you have sent me. I have made you known to them, and will continue to make you known in order that the love you have for me may be in them and that I myself may be in them. (John 17 v 25-26)

This is amazing! The Lord prayed for you 2,000 years ago; and He prays for you in heaven today.

This dynamic is important to notice. Because Jesus is interceding for us, we can pray. And because Jesus is interceding for us, we don't have to pray!

Jesus Himself, sitting next to the Father in heaven, is praying for me and my needs. The Father is going to answer Him, and give Him what He asks for. It isn't critical that I pray—Jesus will ask for what I need. If I forget to pray, or wilfully decide not to pray and then regret it later, I do not need to fear that God wasn't, and isn't, with me or helping me. Jesus was praying even when I wasn't.

The Lord Jesus praying for me, though, also means that I *will* pray. Jesus wants me to enjoy the same relationship He has with God, so He will pray for me to have that relationship. Part of that is for me to pray to my Father as He does.

Prayer, like all the other ways we serve Christ now, is dependent on Jesus' service, and made possible by His service. So prayer, like other ways of serving, is not something we need to do—it is something we are able to do; an opportunity to enjoy, not a chore to endure.

Today, right now, Jesus is serving you by praying.

Jesus sends the Holy Spirit

> I will ask the Father, and he will give you another Counsellor to be with you for ever—the Spirit of truth. The world cannot accept him, because it neither sees him nor knows him. But you know him, for he lives with you and will be in you.
>
> (John 14 v 16-17)

God Himself, the Holy Spirit, lives in every follower of Jesus, because the Lord gives Him to us. Jesus kept the promise that He had made to His disciples on the day of Pentecost, when the Spirit first came to His people (Acts 2 v 1-4). He keeps His promise to us—anyone who turns to Christ as King will "receive the gift of the Holy Spirit", because "the promise is for you and your children and for all who are far off" (v 38, 39)—even for those of us who live hundreds of years and thousands of miles from first-century Jerusalem.

Jesus gives us the Spirit so that "I will not leave you as orphans; I will come to you" (John 14 v 18). He serves us by making sure we are never left alone. The Holy Spirit comes and lives in us. We are, literally, one with Jesus because the Spirit ties us that closely to Him. This is why we are told that we are "in Christ" so much in the New Testament.

This service of Christ helps us when we serve Him. Christ's last words to His disciples, as recorded by Matthew, were:

> All authority in heaven and on earth has been given to me. Therefore go and make disciples of all nations, baptising them in the name of the Father and of the Son and of the Holy Spirit, and teaching them to obey everything I have commanded you. And surely I am with you always, to the very end of the age. (Matthew 28 v 18-20)

The command here is enormous, and intimidating. There they are, just eleven men, most (if not all) of whom have never left Israel. How does the Lord Jesus tell them to serve Him? "Go and make disciples of all nations." Jesus' followers in every age are to go to every nation, community, tribe and group in the world. We are to keep on taking out the good news of Jesus that makes people His followers and teaches them to be obedient disciples.

It is the sort of command that ought to rob the church of all confidence; it is simply too big a task to take on. It is the sort of job that makes you call in sick! Or it would be, except for that promise at the end: "Surely I am with you always". The constant presence of the Lord of the mission is what makes the mission possible. He is with us by His Spirit, who lives in us and makes us one with Him. Where we are, so is Jesus! He asks great things of us; but He never asks us to do them alone.

Today, right now, Jesus is serving you by sending you His Spirit.

Jesus is involved

We see this dynamic in the way the Bible describes Jesus as a Shepherd. Jesus describes Himself as the Good Shepherd twice in John 10. The first time, it is to refer to His greatest act of service for His sheep:

> I am the good shepherd. The good shepherd lays down
> his life for the sheep. The hired hand is not the shepherd
> who owns the sheep. So when he sees the wolf coming, he
> abandons the sheep and runs away. Then the wolf attacks the
> flock and scatters it.   (John 10 v 11-13)

When the sheep are in danger, the shepherd gets between the sheep and the wolf, and he lets fly with his slingshot. If he hits the wolf, the sheep are safe. If he misses, they are safe too, as the wolf can enjoy a juicy shepherd instead of a sheep. Jesus got between us and death, sin and hell. He took them down at the cost of His life.

Jesus goes on, though, to repeat that He is the Good Shepherd, and now it is His ongoing service that He is talking about:

> I am the good shepherd; I know my sheep and my sheep
> know me—just as the Father knows me and I know the
> Father—and I lay down my life for the sheep. I have other
> sheep that are not of this sheep pen. I must bring them also.
> They too will listen to my voice, and there shall be one flock

and one shepherd. The reason my Father loves me is that I
lay down my life—only to take it up again.   (John 10 v 14-17)

Christ lays down His life for His flock, but He will also come
back to life to gather and lead His sheep. This is why a Christian
can, with great confidence and joy, say:

The LORD is my shepherd, I shall not be in want.
He makes me lie down in green pastures,
he leads me beside quiet waters,
he restores my soul.
He guides me in paths of righteousness
for his name's sake.
Even though I walk through the valley of the shadow of
death,
I will fear no evil,
for you are with me;
your rod and your staff,
they comfort me.   (Psalm 23 v 1-4)

Our shepherd has a rod and a staff. A shepherd's staff leads
the sheep. Not having been a sheep, I'm not sure exactly how
they think; but essentially, sheep know that if they keep their
eye on the staff up ahead, and follow where it leads, they will
be safe.

A shepherd's rod has a different purpose to the staff. It is to
prod sheep who are falling behind or wandering off, to draw
them back to safety. When we are falling behind, we can expect
a prod! Jesus won't let us fall back and be destroyed. He will
serve us by disciplining us, sometimes painfully, as well as by
leading us. He is actively involved in forging the path for us.
He is actively involved in leading and poking us into it. He
will work to keep us with Him, even if that means some hard
prods!

This isn't punishment—Jesus has taken all the punishment we will ever deserve. This is loving discipline. When a mother grabs her child's hand and pulls him back firmly as he steps unthinkingly onto a busy road, she isn't punishing him—she's keeping him alive. Jesus' desire is to fill our lives with blessing and to bring us safely through the valley of the shadow of death and into eternal life. If we start to wander away from Him, we are wandering away from blessing and from life. Jesus will call us back. And He will prod us back. He loves us enough to serve us with a staff and a rod.

Today, right now, Jesus is serving you by leading you as your Shepherd.

Jesus is still actively serving us. He serves you each day far more than you serve Him. We are served, not servants. And in fact, He doesn't only serve you *as* you serve Him. He serves you in *letting* you serve Him. We don't often see it like this, but our service is not a down-payment, a drawback, or a drag—it's a gift. A gift from Jesus to us...

10. The gift of serving

We've seen how our "Christian service" can in fact be service of a false god, or service of ourselves. We've seen that Christians are not servants, so much as served; served past and present by the Lord Jesus, making us His friends, His bride, His Father's sons.

But you probably picked up this book to find out about how you can serve without sinking—and most of this book has been about how Jesus serves, not how you serve! That's because the gospel, and the Bible, is not about us; it is about Him. But still, it might seem by this stage that there is no place left for Christians serving Jesus. A Muslim friend once told me that he thought the idea that we are saved from God's anger by God's grace removes the motivation for holiness. He said that he tried to live a holy life because otherwise Allah would judge and punish him. Because I was forgiven, he said, I had no reason to lead a good life or to serve God or others in any way.

I think that we often implicitly agree with him. This is why we talk a lot about what Christians "ought" to do. We say that we're saved by Jesus, but that we ought to be good, ought to read our Bibles, ought to use our gifts for Him, ought to serve, ought to make sacrifices.

Where else can we go? It is all well and good to say, as we have been saying, that Christ serves us. But surely that will lead to a passive church, and create lazy Christians who just lie around and don't do anything? We are the friends and bride of Jesus and the children of God by faith, not by works—won't we take advantage of that and sit around, doing very little, taking no risks and accepting no hardships? Why serve Him at all?

That's what the next two chapters are about.

The best gift

> Which of you fathers, if your son asks for a fish, will give
> him a snake instead? Or if he asks for an egg, will give him a
> scorpion? If you then, though you are evil, know how to give
> good gifts to your children, how much more will your Father
> in heaven give the Holy Spirit to those who ask him!
>
> (Luke 11 v 11-13)

Human fathers are flawed, Jesus says here; but they still "know how to give good gifts" to their children. God is a perfect Father; He, too, knows how to give gifts to us.

God gives different gifts to His people. We are not all given wealth or health, families, foreign holidays, fulfilling careers, and so on. But all God's people are given one identical gift—the best gift He has to give. We are all given His Holy Spirit. As we've already seen, it's through His Spirit that Jesus is with us. It's through the Spirit that we are, and can know we are, friends and the bride and sons:

> You received the Spirit of sonship. And by him we cry, "*Abba*,
> Father." The Spirit himself testifies with our spirit that we are
> God's children. (Romans 8 v 15-16)

The Holy Spirit both makes us children of God, uniting us with our Father, and also reminds us that we are children of God. The Spirit is an amazing gift to us. He brings us into the family of God. Everything we have seen about being friends of Jesus, being His bride, being sons of the Father, all this is given to us, made real for us, by the Holy Spirit. The Spirit is an eternal gift, who keeps on giving. He is the best gift we can ever have, and He is the gift that God has given all of us.

More gifts

The Holy Spirit is the best gift, but He isn't the only gift God has for us. We have a God who loves to give. A God full of generosity, kindness and love, who has some more great gifts to lavish on His children:

> There are different kinds of gifts, but the same Spirit. There are different kinds of service, but the same Lord. There are different kinds of working, but the same God works all of them in all men.
> Now to each one the manifestation of the Spirit is given for the common good ... All these are the work of one and the same Spirit, and he gives them to each one, just as he determines.
> The body is a unit, though it is made up of many parts; and though all its parts are many, they form one body ...
> Now you are the body of Christ, and each one of you is a part of it. And in the church God has appointed first of all apostles, second prophets, third teachers, then workers of miracles, also those having gifts of healing, those able to help others, those with gifts of administration, and those speaking in different kinds of tongues. Are all apostles? Are all prophets? Are all teachers? Do all work miracles? Do all have

gifts of healing? Do all speak in tongues? Do all interpret?
But eagerly desire the greater gifts.

(1 Corinthians 12 v 4-14; v 27-31)

The Spirit, this great gift to us, is also the One through whom the Father gives us other gifts. He loves us, so He gives us gifts to express that love. But did you notice that these gifts are things that we use to serve? If I have the gift of teaching, then "unwrapping" that gift will mean doing some Bible teaching. If I have the gift of helping others, then clearly the way to "play with" it is to help others. In other words, being able to serve in the ways you do is a good gift from your Father. What we sometimes think of as chores to be done, the Father thinks of as gifts to be unwrapped.

But are these actually *good* gifts? Think of the area of Christian service you feel most burdened by, or naturally dislike the most. If having the ability and circumstances to perform that work is God's present to you, wouldn't you like the receipt so you can return it?!

It's one thing to say: *These are good gifts, because they're from God.* But how are they good? Why should we enjoy unwrapping and using them as much as a child enjoys their Christmas presents? Well, we are not merely servants; we are friends—and our Friend has explained to us why these sometimes unwelcome gifts are, in fact, wonderful generosity.

Unity

God made all of us to use our gifts relationally. I know someone who was bought the board game *Monopoly* for Christmas as a child. She shut herself away and played it... on her own! She had a good time—but that is hardly the way to fully enjoy the game!

God's gifts are given to be enjoyed with others. "To each one the manifestation [outward sign] of the Spirit is given for the common good" (1 Corinthians 12 v 7). The idea is that God's people are meant to use their Spirit-given gifts to serve the rest of God's people. They create unity, and they depend on unity. That's why different people have different gifts. It enables us to help one another, and causes us to rely on one another.

So last Sunday, Bill used his teaching gift in the church meeting. That was only possible because several people had used gifts of giving to contribute generously to the church funds, so Bill could be paid as pastor and have the time to prepare his teaching. Meanwhile, Jane had spent a good few hours sorting out the church accounts and bills, so there were lights on and the room was warm. Dave is suffering with bad depression, but took some comfort and hope from the sermon. But he was only there because Steve and Julie took time during the week to use gifts of encouragement and hospitality to hang out with him and help him get to a place where he could bear to be in such a big meeting. But it was good he was there, because Jo brought along a non-Christian friend who is also struggling with depression, so Dave was able to use his gifts of evangelism and wisdom in conversation.

God's gifts do not work by themselves. They rely on the context of the church body. And in needing this unity, they help to create it. They make it obvious to everyone that we need each other. They cut against the individualism of sinful selfishness and make us enjoy being part of Christ's body, the church.

Perhaps next time you are using an ability or circumstance that God has given you to serve someone else, it's worth remembering that the Spirit could have simply given them that time, or money, or upbeat nature, or physical strength, or whatever. He didn't. He chose to give it to you, so that you could give it to them. That's a gift to you, as well as to them.

Christ-likeness

Maybe you read the lists of gifts in the Bible and some of the gifts are clearly good presents, while others you think are best avoided.

After all, some of these gifts sound fine, but what about contributing to the needs of others (Romans 12 v 8)? There's a gift no-one wants! You're in the line and the Holy Spirit is giving out the gifts. Healing goes to someone else, shame... Evangelist does too, that would've been fun... Administrator goes to the person standing next to you, phew. Then He comes to you: Contributing! You see the Evangelist sidling over with a hungry look in his eye and a form in his hand as he begins to tell you of the cost of Bibles and the needs in the mission field. You begin to wonder if the administrator will swap...

The point is that these gifts can feel terribly hard to use, and even harder to love having. Maybe you are faced with a gift you are struggling to enjoy. Whether it is the conviction of the Spirit that it's time to join the new church-planting team, sell your house and buy one in a cheaper area, giving the difference to pay the pastor for the first year. Whether it is that you long to be married and struggle to see singleness as a gift. Whether it is simply that you know it's right to serve in the Sunday School, even though you dread church because of it.

Why should you joyfully use a gift that you didn't ask for and don't want? Why shouldn't you envy the person who has the abilities, the circumstances, the time, the money that you'd have chosen if you were given free pick of God's gifts?

Christ's gifts are good *because they draw us to Him*. He is the greatest treasure we can have, and He will draw us closer and closer to Him.

And He will use our gifts, even (in fact, especially) the harder ones, to do this. So spending week after week with the children in Sunday School, needing to prepare, rarely hearing a sermon, may feel hard. But Jesus can give you love for them. He can give you the grace to get on your knees and plead to love them and to love teaching them. He can give you energy to cut out all those shapes to be stuck on other shapes. And each Sunday, He will stand by your shoulder as you show little (chattering, distracted, infuriating!) people His goodness.

And the closeness to Christ won't only be in the Sunday School room, it will be there when they give testimony to Christ's love as young adults. It will be there on the day Jesus returns and you see a small cluster of people joyfully praising their Lord, and realise with a joy you've never before experienced that it was *your teaching* that God used to save their souls.

If the gift feels bad, we need to unwrap it more and see that it is given to draw us to Christ. If we were only given gifts which enabled us to serve in ways we naturally found easy or fun, we wouldn't learn to depend on Christ, to lean on Christ, to ask Him for help. We need gifts and service that lead us to draw closer to Jesus. That's what a naturally unwanted gift can do, as long as we don't look at it and think that God must be cold-hearted to give us what we didn't ask for.

Hard gifts are good gifts *because they draw us to Christ*. And hard gifts are good gifts *because they make us more like Christ*.

God has chosen us to "be conformed to the likeness of his Son" (Romans 8 v 29). We are being made like Jesus. So if the Spirit has given me the "gift of giving", then He has given it to me so that I can become more like Christ who, "though he was rich, yet for your sakes he became poor, so that you through his poverty might become rich" (2 Corinthians 8 v 9). As I give sacrificially, I am giving like Christ did. I'm becoming more like the person He wants me to be. And I'm showing others what He is like. That is why Christians are able to give cheerfully (9 v 7) even as they give sacrificially.

It is the same with any act of service, because after all, Jesus is the ultimate and greatest Servant of all. When we are mopping the floor to clean up the baby-sick after crèche, that is a good gift! The gift is good not because of what it is, but because of who gives it and what He gives it for. So I think to myself: *Wiping up this sick is, in and of itself, disgusting. But it's a gift from Jesus to make me more like Jesus; and it's a gift from Jesus to enable me to show what He is like. I get to understand Him and to imitate Him. Both of these draw me closer to Him and show His love for me.*

Suddenly, I can see that mopping up vomit is a good gift.

Significance

Third, God's gifts are good presents because there is a significance in using them. When we use a gift Jesus gave us, for His sake, we are serving Him. His cause, "the kingdom of God", is the only thing that will last for ever. You can do something today that will have eternal significance, simply by using an ability or circumstance that Jesus gave you to serve Him.

Jesus once painted a picture of the day He returns. He'll say to those who are His:

> "Come, you who are blessed by my Father; take your inheritance, the kingdom prepared for you since the creation of the world. For I was hungry and you gave me something

to eat, I was thirsty and you gave me something to drink, I
was a stranger and you invited me in, I needed clothes and
you clothed me, I was sick and you looked after me, I was in
prison and you came to visit me."
Then the righteous will answer him, "Lord, when did we see
you hungry and feed you, or thirsty and give you something
to drink? When did we see you a stranger and invite you in,
or needing clothes and clothe you? When did we see you sick
or in prison and go to visit you?"
The King will reply, "I tell you the truth, whatever you did for
one of the least of these brothers of mine, you did for me."

(Matthew 25 v 34-40)

If you make a cup of tea for a friend from church... if you
tidy up to save someone else the bother... if you pop in to see a
struggling church member on your way home... Jesus will count
it as being done for Him, and He will remember it when He
comes back in His glory. What you do matters because you do it
for Jesus, even when you do it for others.

It also matters because it will endure eternally. If we are using
what we have been given to build the kingdom, our work will be
significant for ever.

If any man builds on [Jesus Christ] using gold, silver, costly
stones, wood, hay or straw, his work will be shown for what
it is, because the Day will bring it to light. It will be revealed
with fire, and the fire will test the quality of each man's work.
If what he has built survives, he will receive his reward. If
it is burned up, he will suffer loss; he himself will be saved,
but only as one escaping through the flames. Don't you know
that you yourselves are God's temple and that God's Spirit
lives in you?   (1 Corinthians 3 v 12-16)

We are builders, building on the foundation of Christ. Some
work is burned up; other work endures into eternity. What work

lasts? It is the work that goes into building God's temple, and Paul says that temple is us! The work we do to bring people to Jesus and build them up in Jesus, and the work we do to enable others to do these things, endures for eternity.

This is mindblowing, and completely changes our view of serving Jesus. It means that wherever you are, and whoever you are, whatever you do for Jesus is of eternal significance. In the coming kingdom, you'll be able to see how even the smallest or least impressive service contributed to God's great plan to save His people. You'll see how cleaning up that sick has had eternal significance.

Before you read on, it's worth thinking about the gifts Jesus has given you. Perhaps write them down. What abilities do you have? What time or energy do you have? What opportunities do you have to use those things to serve Him? (Don't think about what you don't have—God knew what He was doing when He gave you the gifts that He did!)

Now for each of these service opportunities, think through how they enable (or would enable, if they're things you're not yet doing) others to lean on you and you to lean on others. Ask yourself how they make you depend on Jesus more; how they make you more like Him; how they enable you to show what He is like to those around you. And for each, say to yourself: *Though I can't always see how, that service is of eternal significance. It will matter long after this world has passed.*

God's gifts are, indeed, good ones.

11. Serving is love

Being friends, the bride, and sons means we are not *compelled* to serve, or obliged to serve. But it's that radical new identity that means that we are *motivated* to serve. It's as we realise who we are through Jesus' service of us that we understand that we don't *have* to serve. But it's also as we realise who we are that we find ourselves *wanting* to serve.

That's because a friend loves. A bride loves. A son loves. And so a friend helps his friend; a bride serves her husband; a son puts himself out for his father. None of them does these things because they have to, but because they want to. They do it because of who they are, and who they are serving.

What if our service of Jesus is a way He gives us to enjoy His love? What if serving Jesus were simply an overflow of love?

Love and obedience

Jesus says: "If you love me, you will obey what I command" (John 14 v 15). This is very simple. However, it is often warped. We sometimes think that obedience and love are the same thing, that you cannot have one without the other. Or we think that obedience leads to love; so if I get on with obeying, the love will come. Yet there are plenty of reasons why I might obey someone that have nothing to do with love. I might obey the government because prison sounds grim, or obey my boss because I want to keep my job, or obey a teacher because I want to do well in an exam. And we've seen that I might obey Jesus for all kinds of reasons that have nothing to do with loving Him!

Where there is love for Christ, there will be obedience; but where there is obedience, there is not necessarily love.

The reason that this sort of obedience=love teaching is attractive is that it makes love something I can achieve. If love is simple obedience, then I can kid myself that I "love" Jesus just by keeping a few rules. I give money to my church. I help clear up after services. I try to be a good husband, father and friend. So I "love" Jesus. "Loving Jesus" is something that I can do.

The Bible undermines this. Paul names the first part of the fruit of the Spirit as "love" (Galatians 5 v 22). The fruit of the Spirit is the characteristics that the Holy Spirit grows in the life of the believer. Loving is not something I can make myself do. It is something the Spirit grows in me.

This is because love is a condition of my heart. It is a deep-running reality, something internal. And I can't just flick it on and off.

So if a friend confides that he is struggling to act Christianly at work because he has demanding, arrogant, unreasonable clients or co-workers, we might reply: *You need to love them.* The problem is that we are telling our friend to do something impossible! We don't realise this, though, because by *love them* we mean: *Be polite to them, bite your tongue, don't think too badly of them.* This isn't love, though. It is niceness (I am awesome at this!).

Pure, Christ-like love is impossible. When Jesus told us to "love your enemies [and] do good to those who hate you" (Luke 6 v 27), He was commanding something impossible for us. Even if we can bring ourselves to do good to those who hate us, we can't make love for them flow from our hearts.

Jesus is not telling us to be obedient. He is telling us to love Him—and then rightly-motivated obedience will flow inevitably and naturally out of us. The origin of that love is the gift of a new heart, given to us by the Holy Spirit, as the Lord God promised through His prophet, Ezekiel:

> I will cleanse you from all your impurities and from all your idols. I will give you a new heart and put a new spirit in you; I will remove from you your heart of stone and give you a heart of flesh. And I will put my Spirit in you and move you to follow my decrees and be careful to keep my laws.
>
> (Ezekiel 36 v 24-27)

The Spirit gives us a new heart, with a new capacity to love, when we become a follower of Jesus. Serving Jesus is the way we express the love for Him which the Spirit causes to well up in our new hearts. It is the natural and inevitable outworking of loving Him. We serve Jesus because we love Him and we naturally want to express that love.

The only right motivation for serving or obeying Christ Jesus is love. It sounds so simple and obvious; but we saw in chapters three and four how easy and natural it is for us to serve for any and every reason other than love.

When we serve in love, everything changes.

Think about an act of service for a moment, maybe something you do in church, at home or at work. Choose something repetitive—a way you serve others every day or each week. Now ask: *If I do that act of service as a way to earn God's love or blessing, or to impress others or be needed by others, what will it do to my heart?* One of two things. It will fill your heart with pride, if you're noticed or needed, or if you consider that now you have deserved God's blessing. Or it will fill it with despondency or bitterness, if you feel you haven't had the praise you deserve, or if God doesn't do for you what you think He should.

Either way, you will not know love. Your heart will be hardened to God. That's what any wrongly-motivated service does. We can be working hard for our church and in doing so hardening our hearts to the Lord of the church.

Now take that same act of service, and ask yourself: *If I do this act as an expression of love for Jesus that is in my heart, what will it do to me?* It will be joyful and satisfying (even if it's hard and tiring). It won't make any difference if it isn't noticed or thanked, or change your standing before your Saviour. Your heart will simply love serving out of love for God. You'll have experienced what it is to have an easy yoke.

This promises that you can find freedom and joy in your service. Service becomes something to cherish, rather than just a chore. It becomes an expression of love.

This has a fundamental implication. If your service of Christ has grown grudging (or stopped happening), you don't need to try to obey more. You need to love more. This means that you don't need to try harder; you need to ask your Father to send His Spirit to work in your heart to make you more loving. You need Him to work in you so that you increasingly enjoy the goodness of Jesus, appreciate the service of Jesus, and let Jesus recapture your heart with His love.

Love makes service joyful and free

Let's look at one example of this loving, free, joyful service. Writing to the church in Corinth, Paul says:

> And now, brothers, we want you to know about the grace
> that God has given the Macedonian churches. Out of the
> most severe trial, their overflowing joy and their extreme
> poverty welled up in rich generosity. For I testify that they
> gave as much as they were able, and even beyond their ability.
> Entirely on their own, they urgently pleaded with us for the
> privilege of sharing in this service to the saints.
>
> (2 Corinthians 8 v 1-4)

Paul was collecting money in Greece for the churches in Jerusalem and Judea because they were suffering from a famine. And the Macedonian churches decided to serve their distant brothers, despite their own "extreme poverty". They showed "rich generosity"—in fact, they "gave ... beyond their ability". And how did they feel about all this? "Overflowing joy."

They are poor, someone asks them for money, they give it away, and their response is joy! This sounds ridiculous at worst, unrealistic at best. We can understand giving happily an amount that doesn't hurt our standard of living; we might imagine giving sacrificially because, well, we know we ought to; but could we really ever give away more than we could afford *and* have overflowing joy? Verse 4 is frankly bizarre to me: they *pleaded* to be able to give their money away.

I have never seen this. I have been in church planting for eight years, and there is never enough money! When I have asked for more, I have never found people pleading to give. I have never had to turn down a giver because they are being too generous. I don't want to give the wrong impression; I have met many wonderfully generous Christians. But I have not met a whole church-full. Usually a few generous, sacrificial people bankroll a church. Here poor churches, as a whole, plead to give more than they can afford to other churches they've never met.

Why? Simply because of "the grace that God has given the Macedonian churches" (v 1). God gave them a grace, a gift. That gift was the opportunity to give their money away.

When we serve Christ, we are not giving Him something; He is giving us something. When you visit a friend from church who is sick, and take her some groceries and stay to clean her house and make supper for her kids, you are serving her and serving Christ. But you are not giving something to Him. You use your time, effort and money to serve your friend, and this is Christ's gift to you.

It might be that you think this is crazy. How does that work? If I do something for someone else, then surely I am giving them something. But I think, in our hearts, we know that this is not the case. When you finish vacuuming your own house, there is a bit of satisfaction, maybe mixed with tiredness. When you finish vacuuming your friend's, there is joy at her pleasure, there is deeper friendship, there is a deeper sense of satisfaction. You are enjoying serving her. You are expressing your love for Jesus and His people. You are living as you were created to live. You are happy. Jesus gave you a gift.

Of course, it doesn't always feel like this. But remember, love does not come from serving; serving flows out of love. And love is God-given; so if we would have sat in a Macedonian pew trying to avoid Paul's eye, giving little or giving grudgingly, the answer is: *ask God for a heart of love.*

Love makes service God-like

Jesus enjoyed serving us. We are told in Psalm 45 v 7 that Jesus, the ultimate King of God's people, was happier than anyone else, anointed with "the oil of joy" above His "companions".

His joy was in serving the one He loved. Jesus loved the Father, and expressed His love in obedience; and this made Him happy.

It's the same for us. In John 13, the night before He goes to the cross, Jesus pictures what He'll do the next day by washing His followers' feet. It is a dirty, humbling, disgusting job to do. It's the job of a servant. And having loved His disciples by serving them, Jesus tells them:

> I have set you an example that you should do as I have done for you ... Now that you know these things, you will be blessed if you do them. (John 13 v 15, 17)

True service of Jesus brings blessing: fulfilment, satisfaction, a sense that we are being the people we have been created to be. But for service to make us full of joy like this, it must be service that springs from love. And this love is given to us as the Spirit restores our hearts, as He shows and reminds us of who we are as friends and the bride and sons. It is the Spirit who makes love real in our experience.

Spirit-given love is what drives real service of the Son. If our service isn't an overflow of this love, it will always tend to fit into one of the categories we explored in chapters three and four. It will always produce emotions of bitterness towards God, or pride in ourselves, or annoyance with others. It will weary and burden us.

When do you feel as though you are serving, but sinking? Where are you working hard, joylessly? Come to Jesus. Ask Him to come to you afresh through His Spirit. Love Him.

And then you'll find that love expressing itself in service. And as you bear that easy yoke, there'll be blessing.

12. Slaves with a Master

In some ways, it would be great to finish the book at the end of the last chapter. You could put the book down, and seeing yourself as a friend of the Boss, the bride of the King, a son of God, served by Christ, you'd lovingly and joyfully get on with using all those gifts of service you've been given.

Except... the Bible *does* call us servants a lot. In fact, it calls us *slaves*. How can this be? I don't call my wife my slave! I don't see my children as my servants! Could it be that those amazing identities we looked at earlier are just ways of papering over the cold, hard truth; that God calls us to slave for Him after all, that the Christian life is (at least until heaven) one of burden and weariness?

It may seem that this chapter is going to undermine the whole theme of the book; but in fact, thinking about our slavery will help us pull everything we've seen so far together. We need to figure out what it means to be a slave when we are a son.

What is your master like?

In his letters, Paul often referred to himself as a servant of Christ (eg: Romans 1 v 1; Philippians 1 v 1; Titus 1 v 1). So did Peter and

James (2 Peter 1 v 1; James 1 v 1). This was a strong statement, because the Greek word we tend to translate "servant", *douloi*, really means "slave".

Paul was describing his relationship with Jesus as slavery to a readership that was very familiar with the institution. We're familiar with it, too, but in a slightly different way. Our perception of slavery is shaped by the brutal, murderous horrors of the Atlantic slave trade, where men and women were regarded as mere property, sub-humans with no more rights than cattle and treated considerably worse. But in the world of the New Testament, slavery was not always like that. A Roman or Hebrew slave could own and earn money, property and even their own slaves. To be a slave could give you great power—few free men would cross a slave of the emperor.

That's not to say that first-century slavery was a good thing. While they may not have been subjected to violent kidnapping, barbaric shipping and then harsh plantation labour, most slaves lived very poorly. If you were a slave, your master could trade you, beat you, injure you or force you to obedience in back-breaking and harsh work.

Your master *could* do that. But that didn't mean your master *would*. Across the ages, the key element that defines an experience of slavery has always been the same. *It all depends on what your master is like.* Most slavery was brutal because most masters were brutal. It's the character of the master that defines the life of the slave.

Who is your master?

Why does any of this ancient practice matter to 21st-century free western people, though? Because the Bible says something very shocking about everyone, including us. It says that we have to have a master. It says that we are slaves. We will serve someone.

This is the consistent picture across the Bible. Just one example of many is found Matthew 6 v 24, where Jesus says:

> No-one can serve two masters. Either he will hate the one
> and love the other, or he will be devoted to the one and
> despise the other. You cannot serve both God and Money.

You can't serve two masters, but Jesus assumes that you will serve *one*. Serving no-one is impossible.

We will be slaves. We were created to serve. This sounds strange to us—we live in a world that values freedom highly, so we think that the ultimate good life is to be totally free. But when we stop and think about it, we realise that none of us are actually completely free. We all long for happiness, love, security and satisfaction, and we will serve whoever or whatever we think will give us these good things, these blessings. We'll give things up for this person or thing. We'll work hard to get it or keep it. We'll worry about having it. We'll daydream about it. We serve it. We are free to choose what we serve, but we are not free to choose whether we will serve.

The Bible calls this idolatry—when we serve someone or something that is not God as though it was God, the bringer of ultimate blessings and our greatest need. This is what Jesus is getting at when He talks about either serving God or Money. If we serve money, we have made money—a good thing—into an idol—a "god" thing.

Take Scrooge, the famously stingy anti-hero of Charles Dickens' *A Christmas Carol*. He served Money. Money was his god, and he made great sacrifices to it—he gave up friendships, love and family out of love for his god. He subjected his body to hardship, living in cold, small rooms so he could have more of his god. And he became like the god he worshipped—cold, hard and uncaring.

We all know people who worship Money. Often, we know them very well, because not all of Money's worshippers are like Scrooge. Some of them are like me, living in a four-bedroom house but day-dreaming about saving enough to get the kitchen done or moving to the five-bedroom place in the next street. I am wondering if the blessing of having an iPad is worth putting that off for.

I like money; it makes me feel I am secure. It enables me to face the future with confidence. It makes me feel comfortable. I like it, so I am tempted to work hard to get more of it, to serve Money for the blessings it brings. If I have to cut some corners to get some more, perhaps I will. If I have to see the kids a bit less to get more in the bank, it's a price worth paying. (After all, they need money too, don't they? We can worship Money as a family.)

We were made to serve. If you are not a slave of Christ, then you will be a slave to an idol—to fashion, career, family, beauty, money, status or a thousand other little gods. We look to these gods to tell us we matter, that we are loved. In return, we sacrifice for them—our time, resources and relationships are laid on their altars.

Every moment of our lives we are serving something. If you're not a follower of Jesus, what are you serving? And if you are a Christian, think back to the last time you disobeyed Jesus. At that point, what were you serving instead? What were you looking to to provide joy, satisfaction, comfort or security, at the price of disobeying Christ?

Cold masters

The great tragedy of idolatry is that idols are masters who promise us much, and give us nothing. We slave for our master, and in return he gives us—precisely zero. If we look to idols to find hope, meaning, joy, love and peace, we either kid ourselves or we despair. Slavery to idols is miserable and self-destroying.

Let's look at Money again. Money promises security. If you have Money, you can protect yourself against the fears of life. You can buy food, clothes, a house. You can pay the bills. If your car breaks, Money will fix it. If you get ill, Money can get you the best treatment. If you lose something, Money and his co-idol, Insurance, can make sure you get it back.

Money becomes your hope. But Money will disappoint. This was the point of the warnings Scrooge was given about Christmases to come—Money would let him down. This is not just a story. You see people who use Money to buy themselves a legacy, a building or monument that will go on beyond them. Sometimes you get the impression they are seeking for immortality. But their idol will disappoint them. They will not live beyond the grave. Money cannot buy eternal life.

And even this side of death, Money doesn't truly deliver blessings now. If you are serving Money to buy security, how much do you need? What would happen if you got ill? Or if there were an economic depression and you lost your job? Or your spouse left you and got the wealth? Or the banks collapsed?

Or if you're chasing Money because it will satisfy you to have it, how much will you need to buy you happiness if your greatest love gets seriously sick? Or if you have plenty, but look round and realise that you sacrificed your relationships and your reputation on its altar and cannot get them back?

Money cannot deliver what it promises—in this life or the next. No idol-master does.

The freedom of slavery

If we're all slaves, how can we be free? Only by being slaves to a Master who offers us freedom. It can only be found in slavery to Christ. This sounds like a contradiction to us, but not to God. Through Paul, He says simply:

> You have been set free from sin and have become slaves to
> righteousness.   (Romans 6 v 18)

The character of the master we serve defines the life that we live. Freedom is only possible if we serve a master who offers it. Back in the second chapter we looked at Matthew 11 v 28-30, where Jesus said:

> Come to me, all you who are weary and burdened, and I will
> give you rest. Take my yoke upon you and learn from me, for
> I am gentle and humble in heart, and you will find rest for
> your souls. For my yoke is easy and my burden is light.

Jesus promises to give us rest, to take all our burdens. This is the freedom that God offers. It is freedom from anything that weighs us down: freedom from fear, guilt, shame and sin, from loneliness and despair. It is freedom from idols. It is freedom to be the people we were created to be, and would love to be, and are often striving to be. But it is not an independent, autonomous freedom. It is to be yoked, to have a Master, to be a slave.

But what a Master! Christ is gentle and humble. He is a kind Friend, a loving Husband, a wonderful Brother. He is the Master with whom we find real security and true satisfaction, for this life and beyond.

We are not free not to be a servant. So when we don't serve Christ at all, we're still serving—we're serving a different "god". And when we serve but with wrong motives, we're serving a false god too—worshipping a god who says we must earn his help, or worshipping the idol of popularity, or busy-ness, and so on.

The question each of us answers is not: *Will you have a master?* It is: *Who is your master?* It will be Jesus, or it will be an idol. "A man cannot serve two masters."

Trust your Master

Freedom and blessing are found in being a slave. We already saw the Macedonian church—they were the guys who pleaded to give generously to help out other churches during a famine. They were the people living in poverty who enjoyed being generous when they couldn't afford it.

They were free. They were free from fear of not having enough. They were free from needing money so that others would respect them. They were free from the need to find their pleasure in what they could buy. They were free because they served Jesus, not Money. They were free because they had a Master who they trusted to supply their needs; a Master who respected them so highly they didn't need the respect of others; a Master who was such a joy to know that they didn't need the pleasures that Money could offer.

They were free from idolatry of Money. They were free because they were slaves.

This makes a huge difference to how we respond to the circumstances of life. Paul, as a *doulos* of Christ, shows us what it means to be free from worshipping the idols of wealth, or comfort, or self-reliance:

I know what it is to be in need, and I know what it is to have
plenty. I have learned the secret of being content in any and
every situation, whether well fed or hungry, whether living in
plenty or in want. I can do everything through him who gives
me strength.   (Philippians 4 v 12-13)

Because he knows Jesus, Paul is happy if he has lots or little.
Because Jesus is his Master, he lives for Him. He sacrifices
everything for Him. He serves Him, no matter what the cost,
because he knows that he already has what is most precious,
Jesus Himself:

Five times I received from the Jews the forty lashes minus
one. Three times I was beaten with rods, once I was stoned,
three times I was shipwrecked, I spent a night and a day in
the open sea, I have been constantly on the move. I have
been in danger from rivers, in danger from bandits, in
danger from my own countrymen, in danger from Gentiles;
in danger in the city, in danger in the country, in danger
at sea; and in danger from false brothers. I have laboured
and toiled and have often gone without sleep; I have known
hunger and thirst and have often gone without food; I have
been cold and naked. Besides everything else, I face daily the
pressure of my concern for all the churches.

                                    (2 Corinthians 11 v 25-28)

Paul's service was longer, harder, harsher than mine or yours
will ever be. How do you endure that and be content? It can only
be if your God is Christ. To be content with that lot, you must
have a Master worth following. You must have a Master worth
everything. You must have a Master who loves you hugely and
gives you everything you could need or want, a Master who gives
you Himself in love.

So a Christian is a servant. Ultimately, we have a Master and
we obey Him. It is not our place to tell Him when we think

He's wrong; or when we should be allowed to compromise; or how He ought to let us be more comfortable; or which of His commands we're going to downgrade to guidelines. We are not the Master; He is. We must never forget that He is a good, loving, serving Master, but equally we mustn't forget that He is nevertheless a Master.

Jesus is more than your Master

So we are slaves, after all. This is a good thing. But it raises a difficult question for us (or rather, for me!). This idea of being happy slaves conflicts with the culture we live in, but doesn't it also conflict with this book?! We have spent a lot of time seeing that we are people who are served by Jesus, rather than those who serve Jesus. Surely this is contradicted by this idea that we were created to be slaves?

The answer to the dilemma of how we are slaves as well as those served by Christ is to get the order right. If we think of ourselves primarily as slaves, then we will never believe that we are loved unless we are performing well and working hard. If we see ourselves as friends of the Boss, bride of the King, sons of the Father, and only *in that context* as slaves of our Master, then we will enjoy our slavery, shaped by those prior relationships.

This is how we make sense of Paul calling himself a slave even after Jesus said that He called His disciples friends and no longer servants. Paul knew he was one with Christ, and in that love and closeness there is security in being bought, being owned, being entirely under the direction of such a kind Master. We are not slaves instead of being sons. We are not slaves to earn the right to be sons. We are sons, who are happy slaves of God.

So we serve long and hard and joyfully and sacrificially and lovingly and obediently, working for the Master who is our Friend, our Husband, our Brother. Because of who we are, we can serve Christ *and* keep our joy. In fact, we can serve Christ and *increase* our joy.

13. The joy of serving Jesus

What shall we do?

I often read a book about an aspect of the Christian life and feel challenged and encouraged by it. I then close the book, put it down, and get on with the next thing on the to-do list, without praying and thinking about it any more.

The Holy Spirit uses books to challenge and encourage us, but He also uses them to change us. So I want to finish this book by thinking about a couple of questions: *What will we do?* And: *Who will we be?* In other words: *What difference will this book make?*

It is helpful to look at ourselves a little bit, then to look at Jesus a lot. You probably did the first as you read through the chapters early on about the reasons why we often serve Christ. Perhaps you were particularly struck by one or two of those skewed motives as you spotted them in your own heart. A simple way to do a little self-diagnosis might be to compare the time you spend serving Jesus in obvious ways (doing stuff at church, say) to the time you spend praying. How much we pray is a very good indicator of our spiritual health. Robert Murray M'Cheyne, a nineteenth-century pastor, said:

> A man is what he is on his knees before God, and nothing more.

He was right. Most of the reasons we serve Christ (apart from dependent love!) don't require us to pray. So a good way of spotting wrong-hearted service is that it will lack prayer.

This is all of us, isn't it? We don't need to fear because of this—we are served by Jesus because of how much He loves us, not because of how well we love or serve Him. If I am feeble in my praying (and I am), it doesn't change the warmth and love the Father has for me. He loves me because Christ died for me, not because I pray to Him.

We don't need to fear, but we do need to change—not so that God will love us, but so that we can enjoy that love more fully.

Now let's turn to Jesus. The way to stop defining ourselves by our service of Christ is simply to grasp more fully how He has served, and is serving, us. If you are not a Christian, then Jesus makes an offer in Matthew 11 v 28:

> Come to me, all you who are weary and burdened, and I will give you rest.

A life with Jesus is rest. It is a life where all we strive for—love, recognition, meaning, significance—is given to us as a free, unconditional gift, as we are befriended, married and adopted. If you are not a Christian, then Jesus is offering this to you. Why not take Him up on it?

If you are a Christian, then Jesus makes you the same offer, in the same verse! If you feel burdened and wearied by service, then something has gone wrong. If you wish you could have a break... if you look forward to not having to serve anymore...

if you are sinking... then something has gone wrong. Christ promises to give us rest. We will enjoy this rest fully on the day when He comes back, but we—you—can begin to enjoy it *now*. The circumstances of life can be extremely hard, but He gives rest in them. Rest from needing to achieve, to succeed, to be noticed, to be the best. Not rest *from* serving, but rest *in* joyful serving.

How do you turn to Christ? You can just ask Him. Open the Bible and read it for the joy of hearing from Him. Listen to music, eat food, enjoy a pint, and feel grateful that this is the life He gives you.

Then turn to your service. What are you doing that makes it harder for you to love and enjoy knowing Jesus? Very carefully, prayerfully, and talking it through with Christian friends—remembering that there is nothing that Jesus needs from you, that His mission does not depend on you—ask the question: *Should I stop serving in this area for now?*

Then think about what you are doing to serve Christ that you don't think you should stop—your job, perhaps, or your family responsibilities, or a church commitment you are sure Jesus has called you to. What might it look like to enjoy this as a good gift from your Husband? How will it change if you see it as a privileged role in the family business? How can you pray about this?

Next time you're doing a particular act of service, perhaps try asking yourself these questions:

- *What is the wrong motivation I'll be most tempted to have here?*

- *How does being a friend and the bride of Jesus and a son of God motivate me here?*

- *How is this particular service a gift from God? How is He letting me be part of His work? How am I helping His people? How am I becoming more like His Son?*

- *What will happen if I forget that I am also God's slave?*

After serving (or, if it's more helpful for you, before or during a specific area of serving), you could pray something like this:

> *Lord Jesus, Thank You that You have served me on the cross.*
> *Thank You that You are serving me now.*
> *Thank You that you have made me Your friend, Your bride, and a child of our Father.*
> *Thank You for the gift of being able to serve You in this way.*
> *Please show me and forgive me for any wrong motives, and please send me Your Spirit to increase my right motives by increasing my love.*
> *Please help me to do this act of service humbly, rightly, for You.*
> *And please remind me that I'm a Christian because You serve me, not because I serve You. Amen.*

Who shall we be?

We have already thought about Jesus' wonderful story about the two sons and the loving father a fair bit, because it's so helpful to us in appreciating how God relates to us. We're going to finish with it.

> Jesus continued: "There was a man who had two sons. The younger one said to his father, 'Father, give me my share of the estate.' So he divided his property between them."
>
> (Luke 15 v 11-12)

Everyone in the world is one of the two sons. Some of us are lazy and feel entitled. We want the father's stuff, and we want to use it to party. Some of us are like the older brother. As we've seen, he is more subtle, but really he wants the same thing. He is serving his father because he wants the stuff too, so he serves simply for what's in it for him—he doesn't love the father either. It's unsurprising that, when the bad younger brother comes home, the older brother is... working hard, of course!

> Meanwhile, the older son was in the field. When he came near the house, he heard music and dancing. So he called one of the servants and asked him what was going on. "Your brother has come," he replied, "and your father has killed the fattened calf because he has him back safe and sound."
>
> The older brother became angry and refused to go in. So his father went out and pleaded with him. But he answered his father, "Look! All these years I've been slaving for you and never disobeyed your orders. Yet you never gave me even a young goat so I could celebrate with my friends. But when this son of yours who has squandered your property with prostitutes comes home, you kill the fattened calf for him!"
>
> (Luke 15 v 25-30)

He is burning with rage because his little brother doesn't serve; he wastes and abuses, yet he still gets everything the father has to give. You know, I feel so much empathy for the older brother. As a very polite, British guy, I am far too well-mannered to shout and sulk like him, but inside I'm much the same. I feel that I work hard week after week for God, and other people get such an easy ride from Him. When I see people at church who don't really seem to do anything, I partly envy them and partly resent them.

When I think of all the work I do, and the hours I put in, the idea that God loves them and blesses them exactly the same amount as me... well, it grates a little.

This older brother portrays many Christians who are the hardest-serving members of their churches. Since He captures what is in my heart, I wonder if Jesus here describes the feelings of many other pastors, elders, deacons; and maybe your feelings, too.

The good news is that Jesus came to save older brothers as well as younger brothers, to invite us in to know His love, and to respond to His loving generosity in loving obedience. But the final twist in this story is: we are not told what the older brother ended up doing. The story ends with the father inviting his elder son into the house and into a relationship with him which is based on love, kindness, acceptance and forgiveness—the same relationship his younger son is enjoying, along with his steak.

But... *did the older brother go in?*

Imagine the next day. The father asks his two sons to come and help harvest the barley field. The younger son springs up with joy. He smiles. He is amazed that he can enjoy his father's love as a son. He relishes the work of swinging his scythe for the father who loves him so much.

This is Christian service—it makes you smile. It's an easy yoke.

But what about the older brother? Does he stay on his own, on the outside, hanging around the side of the field, resentful and angry, hating his father's love and forgiveness? Does he go to work for himself—determined to earn his status, his inheritance, desperate to hear his father say: *I love your brother, but I love you more, you hard-working, diligent, deserving man. I know I forgave him, but real sons work hard. Have some extra gifts. Hey, servants, look at the example this son of mine is setting you.*

Or, like his brother, does he smile? Does he smile because for the first time he has realised that he can work for the sheer joy of being with his dad and his brother? Does he smile because he realises that he doesn't need to earn the father's love—he has it already; because he understands that he doesn't need to earn the father's goats—they're all his already. Will he smile as he serves, smile because he's a son, working for his father, working hard, working long, with his dad, for his dad, loved by and loving his dad. Does he smile? Will he smile?

Do you? Will you?

Thank you...

... to the members of *The Plant* in Manchester and Salford, and *BroadGrace*, Norfolk. You have helped and shown me how to love serving Christ in His church.

... to Rob Iveson and Mike Reeves. Your friendship has been the context for lots of my growth in Christ and my delight in talking theologically. You guys are friends beyond any a man like me deserves.

... to Carl Laferton, my editor at The Good Book Company as well as a friend. It has been great to work with you on this book, serving Christ together joyfully, and seeing how different gifts combine to give a better result.

... to Steve and Hannah Michael (and others who think my idealistic vision of rota-less church where everyone enjoys serving is somewhat unrealistic) for encouraging me to write this book and for being great, wise friends who always have our backs.

... to the men and women of Acts 29 Europe. You encourage me to pursue Christ with delight and commitment. I am humbled to be part of such a network of church planters who die to self and live for Christ with such joy.

... to my wife, Flick, and children, Daisy and Eliza. I love being the head of our family, and your generous love for me is a constant lesson in the glorious love of the greatest family, Father, Son and Spirit.

Eternity Changes Everything
Stephen Witmer

This book will thrill you with the difference that eternity makes to us right now. It excites us about what life after death is like, and inspires us to live more contented, patient, loving lives today. If you've ever thought heaven should make more of a difference to you, this is a book to read.

"Reading this is like enjoying a coffee with a new friend as he shares the secret of the universe with you."

Jared Wilson, pastor and author of "Gospel Wakefulness"

"This has hugely shifted my outlook. It will change lives. Make sure you read it." *John Hindley, pastor and author of "Serving without Sinking"*

Look out for...

- **Compared to Her:** How to experience true contentment (for women) *by Sophie de Witt*
- **The Heart of Singleness:** How to be single and satisfied (for women) *by Andrea Trevenna*
- **Purity is Possible:** How to be free of fantasy, porn and guilt *by Helen Thorne* (out October 2014)
- **Get over the Painline:** How to talk about Jesus to today's world *by Rico Tice* (out early 2015)

Order from your local Good Book website:

UK & Europe: www.thegoodbook.co.uk • US & Canada: www.thegoodbook.com
Australia: www.thegoodbook.com.au • New Zealand: www.thegoodbook.co.nz

thegoodbook
COMPANY

Opening up the Bible

At The Good Book Company, we are dedicated to helping Christians and local churches grow. We believe that God's growth process always starts with hearing clearly what He has said to us through His timeless word—the Bible.

Ever since we opened our doors in 1991, we have been striving to produce resources that honour God in the way the Bible is used. We have grown to become an international provider of user-friendly resources to the Christian community, with believers of all backgrounds and denominations using our Bible studies, books, evangelistic resources, DVD-based courses and training events.

We want to equip ordinary Christians to live for Christ day by day, and churches to grow in their knowledge of God, their love for one another, and the effectiveness of their outreach.

Call us for a discussion of your needs or visit one of our local websites for more information on the resources and services we provide.

UK & Europe: www.thegoodbook.co.uk
North America: www.thegoodbook.com
Australia: www.thegoodbook.com.au
New Zealand: www.thegoodbook.co.nz

UK & Europe: 0333 123 0880
North America: 866 244 2165
Australia: (02) 6100 4211
New Zealand (+64) 3 343 1990